D1271705

STRATEGIC
BANKRUPTCY

STRATEGIC BANKRUPTCY

How Corporations and Creditors Use
Chapter 11 to Their Advantage

KEVIN J. DELANEY

ST. PHILIP'S COLLEGE LIBRARY

UNIVERSITY OF CALIFORNIA PRESS
BERKELEY LOS ANGELES OXFORD

University of California Press
Berkeley and Los Angeles, California

University of California Press, Ltd.
Oxford, England

© 1992 by
Kevin J. Delaney

Library of Congress Cataloging-in-Publication Data
Delaney, Kevin J., 1960–
    Strategic bankruptcy : how corporations and creditors use
Chapter 11 to their advantage / Kevin J. Delaney.
        p.   cm.
    Includes bibliographical references and index.
    ISBN 0-520-07358-4 (alk. paper)
    1. Corporations—United States—Finance—Case studies.
    2. Strategic planning—United States—Case studies.
    3. Bankruptcy—United States—Case studies. I. Title
HG4061.D45   1992
658.1'6—dc20   91-22489
                                                          CIP

Printed in the United States of America
1 2 3 4 5 6 7 8 9

The paper used in this publication meets the minimum
requirements of American National Standard for Information
Sciences—Permanence of Paper for Printed Library Materials,
ANSI Z39.48-1984. ⊗

*To Susan, Connor, Doreen
Delaney, and the memory of
my father, Jim Delaney*

Contents

Acknowledgments   ix

Introduction   1

1. Bankruptcy: From "Broken Bench" to "Fad   11
   of the Year"

2. Theories of Corporate Bankruptcy   37

3. The Manville Corporation: Solving Asbestos   60
   Liability through Bankruptcy

4. Continental Airlines: Using Bankruptcy to   82
   Abrogate Union Contracts

5. Texaco: Using Bankruptcy to Frustrate a   126
   Business Rival

6. Bankruptcy as Strategy: Avoiding Financial   160
   Burden and Shifting Financial Risk

References   191

Index   205

Acknowledgments

Many people helped me formulate the ideas in this book. Michael Schwartz, my dissertation advisor, was supportive of my idea to study corporate bankruptcy in my earliest days in graduate school. Mark Granovetter helped me understand economics and economic sociology, Jim Rule faithfully read and commented on this book as it progressed, and David Gray Carlson of Benjamin Cardozo Law School kept me straight on legal matters. Lee Clarke, Davita Glasberg, Harvey Molotch, and Gerry Turkel all read the entire manuscript and provided comments that improved the final product.

My best friends in graduate school, Rick Eckstein and Debra Swoboda, can be found throughout this book. Our many conversations and our study group provided ideas and sustenance. I could not have done this without them. Patrick Shannon was invaluable in providing legal articles about business bankruptcy and in assembling the book. Naomi Schneider and Amy Klatzkin of the University of California Press helped shape this book, and Peter Dreyer performed a wonderful copyediting job.

A host of others read and commented on my work and I wish to thank them: Paul Attewell, Steve Cohen, Lewis Coser, Lyle Hallowell, Cheryl Laz, Chris Nippert Eng, David Halle, Beth Mintz, Mark Mizruchi, Charles Perrow, Susan Silbey, Magali Sarfatti Larson, Milagros Peña, and Ronnie Steinberg. I especially want to thank all of my colleagues at Temple University who helped me survive a faculty strike, the birth of my first child, and the completion of this book—all of which occurred at the same time.

The Delaney and Korman families provided much support and love. I only wish my Dad were still here to see this. Parking cars at North Hills Country Club, working at the Water District, and caddying on weekends was never easy. I hope this book is some small tribute to your hard work and generosity. I know you would be proud of me.

I owe my greatest thanks to Susan Korman for sticking with me through the difficult years of graduate school and completing this book. Thanks also to my new son, Connor, for teaching me how to complete a book in ten-minute intervals. He has provided me with a new sense of joy.

Introduction

In December 1986, I spent many days sitting through hearings in a lower Manhattan bankruptcy court. The courtroom was filled with scores of lawyers and financial experts discussing capitalization rates, valuation ratios, depreciation values, and other technical financial measurements. As I sat listening to the estimates of the worth of the asbestos manufacturer Johns-Manville, I thought about the man sitting right next to me on the wooden court bench. He was having difficulty breathing through an oxygen mask. On that day at the federal courthouse, he was the only visible reminder of what these technical proceedings were all about. He was dying of asbestosis.

Later I asked him what he thought about the bankruptcy proceeding. He told me: "I'm not sure I really understood all those numbers. I just hope we [asbestos victims] finally get something before we die. We've been through so much. I guess they [Manville managers] had no other choice [than declaring bankruptcy]." The bankruptcy court would later decide his fate and the fate of others injured by Manville's asbestos products.

In June 1983, Continental Airlines' senior vice president for flight operations jotted down some notes during a meeting at which the airline's labor troubles were discussed: "I don't believe we can get these [labor] concessions on a voluntary, persuasive basis. We must get an [an] awfully big stick. ... Most effective stick might be Chapter 11" (court testimony, *In re* Continental Airlines, 3 Bankr. L. Rep. [CCH] [Bankr. S.D. Tex. 1984], and Murphy 1986, 223).

Three months later, Continental declared bankruptcy and abrogated its labor contracts with its unions. Continental's CEO, Frank Lorenzo, began referring to the company as "the new Continental" and to any employee working for the firm after its bankruptcy as a "founding employee" (see Continental Airlines, annual report, 1983). One of the "founding employees" at "the new Continental" found his salary immediately reduced from $45,000 to $30,000 (*New York Times* [hereafter cited as *NYT*], September 24, 1984, D1), and a ticket agent came to work after the Chapter 11 filing and found that her hourly wage had been cut from $10 to $7.50 per hour (*NYT*, September 6, 1985, D2).

Employees wondered how the company could violate labor law without penalty. Union officials complained bitterly that Lorenzo had unilaterally broken legally negotiated contracts. But pro-management observers countered that Lorenzo simply had no choice—he responded to a set of financial conditions beyond his control. Lorenzo was later hailed by *Fortune* magazine as one of America's "most fascinating business people" (January 5, 1987, 72) and as "an imaginative entrepreneur" (February 17, 1986, 72).

In 1984, a Texas jury ruled that Texaco had illegally interfered with Pennzoil's agreement to acquire Getty Oil. The jury awarded Pennzoil $10.53 billion in damages, the largest court award in history. Texaco refused to pay the award, despite the fact that it had $35 billion in assets and approximately $13 billion in equity. Instead, Texaco declared bankruptcy. Pennzoil charged that Texaco was using bankruptcy to force Pennzoil to accept a lower award. As *Time* magazine reported at the time, "the U.S. was faced with the spectacle of a healthy corporation sheltering under laws ostensibly intended for the weak and the ailing" (*Time*, April 27, 1988). The Texas jury probably wondered why it had spent so many days in the courtroom listening to testimony if its decision could be rendered ineffective through a bankruptcy filing.

What is happening in bankruptcy court? We usually think of bankruptcy as something bad—a place that managers try to avoid. Scores of popular books with titles like *Turnaround: Avoid Bankruptcy and Revitalize Your Company* (Freiermuth 1989) counsel managers on how to steer clear of what is depicted as the ultimate business disaster. According to popular belief, bankruptcy occurs when management's plans go sour. As Freiermuth puts it: "Texaco, Bank of America, LTV, A. H. Robins, . . . mere mention of the names of corporate giants . . . evokes a certain image of what can happen to a business when the best-laid plans do not develop as expected" (1989, introduction).

But is this true? Do managers avoid bankruptcy and only accept it when all options are exhausted? Is bankruptcy always an anathema to "good business"? In this book, I shall show that profound changes have occurred in our economic, political, legal, and organizational landscape. Bankruptcy has become a strategic, political device used by large corporations and commercial creditors. Recent cases suggest that firms are beginning to view bankruptcy, not as something to be avoided, but as another weapon in the corporate arsenal.

Consider some recent bankruptcies. Manville declared bankruptcy to resolve the liability problem created by its harmful asbestos products, despite the fact that it had over $2 billion in assets. A. H. Robins, notwithstanding apparent financial vigor, entered Chapter 11 to create a payment scheme for women injured by its Dalkon Shield intrauterine device. Continental Airlines and Eastern Air Lines, both led by Frank Lorenzo, coupled bankruptcy filings with the abrogation of all of their labor contracts. Texaco, one of the nation's most profitable oil companies, entered bankruptcy to reduce a court-imposed damage award. LTV, a major steel producer, tried to shift the obligation of providing pension funds to retirees to the federal government through bankruptcy. Numerous smaller companies have declared bankruptcy to avoid cleaning up toxic waste sites. These cases

ST. PHILIP'S COLLEGE LIBRARY

challenge the notion that bankruptcy is contrary to "good business." Instead, it appears that corporations or creditors invoke bankruptcy to achieve a variety of organizational or political goals. Moreover, the usual arbiters of economic health—banks, large insurance companies, bond-rating agencies, and investment bankers—increasingly share the view that bankruptcy is legitimate business strategy.

In this book, I analyze three of the largest of these cases: Manville, Continental, and Texaco. I plan to show that each firm filed for bankruptcy *only* to accomplish a financial or political objective that it had tried unsuccessfully to achieve through more routine processes. All parties to these cases recognized and operated on the assumption that this limited objective was all that was being pursued. Liquidation of the firm was thus not considered a serious option.

You will see that these companies spent incredible resources and public relations efforts to show their customers and suppliers that they were not "really bankrupt." Perhaps they were more right than we realized. I shall illustrate through these examples that companies can "manufacture" or "construct" a claim to bankrupt status through creative accounting, interpreting the terms *liability* and *assets* in novel ways, separating company assets from those of a subsidiary, or shifting assets from one corporate entity to another. I argue that terms such as *asset, liability, insolvent,* and *bankrupt* are far from concrete and objective but instead are subjective and open to competing interpretations.

Oddly, academic theories of bankruptcy have missed the significance of these changes. The assumption that bankruptcy is a financial state of affairs that managers loathe still dominates these theories. There has been a tendency to treat bankruptcy as managerial *reaction* rather than an *action*. Because these theories ignore the possibility of bankruptcy being a strategy, we are left with a functionalist view of the bankruptcy process: firms enter bankruptcy when they have no other choice. In this study, I turn the assumption of accepted bankruptcy theory on its head. Rather than viewing

ST. PHILIP'S COLLEGE LIBRARY

bankruptcy as something that is avoided, I consider the possibility that creditors or corporations may choose bankruptcy as a strategy.

While academic theories of bankruptcy seem trapped by their assumptions, some journalists have noted the increasing use of bankruptcy as a strategy (*Newsday*, April 14, 1987, 43). Unfortunately, these accounts are limited in their consideration of other powerful organizations in this strategic decision-making. Large insurance companies, commercial banks, auditors, and bond-rating agencies all play key roles in the business crises I analyze in this book. These institutional actors continually constrain and shape the options available to management at any given time. While I plan to show that these bankruptcy filings result from strategic decision-making rather than being passive or "natural" responses to market factors, I also argue that we can only understand the choices after accounting for the actions of a wide array of organizations. Thus, viewing the actions of the managers of these firms as either devious or heroic (as many journalists did) misses the fact that other large institutions like financial creditors, insurers, the federal government, and the court have been integral parties to this decision-making.

If I am right that corporations and creditors are coming to view bankruptcy as a strategic weapon, this finding holds wide-ranging implications for the role of the bankruptcy process in society. According to existing theories, bankruptcy is a crucial mechanism in the national economy. It is said to operate both as a neutral forum to collect debt in a fair way and as a neutral market mechanism that discriminates between inefficient firms (which are liquidated) and efficient firms (which are reorganized and continue operating). This book challenges both of these assertions. Despite technical jargon that gives the appearance of objectivity, I view bankruptcy as a political process. As such, we should not be surprised that large organizational players use their legal and societal power to dominate the process. Bankruptcy is about the allocation of scarce resources. In each of the cases discussed, I chart who won and lost in this allocation. As will be apparent, I question the neutrality of the process.

The Manville, Continental, and Texaco cases involved sharp conflicts between powerful organizations or coalitions of interests: corporations, financial institutions, insurance companies, auditors, health victims, and organized labor. Thus, they provide an opportunity to address important theoretical debates in the areas of economic and political sociology, organizational analysis, the sociology of business, and the sociology of law, as well as bankruptcy analysis. Bankruptcy provides an arena in which to assess the power of competing groups during corporate crises. I hope this study adds to our understanding of how a business crisis is brought about and what types of organizations exercise decisive roles in creating business crises.

Understanding business bankruptcy will also help us understand the larger question of how firms and "the market" interact. Bankruptcy theories are dominated by a market model. Corporations are portrayed as having little impact on the market; they simply react to conditions presented by "the larger business environment." Perhaps this is an apt description of a small firm that has little power to affect the market.[1] But, as I shall show, large corporations and commercial creditors have the power to shape what we refer to as "the market." In this study, I detail the levers of power available to corporations and creditors to precipitate or forestall bankruptcy.

"The market" is not an amorphous entity but is made up of lenders, suppliers, and shareholders, many of which have long-standing relationships with their corporate clients. I shall show how corporations, auditors, and creditors play decisive roles in shaping balance-sheet data for strategic advantage. This study suggests, then, that organizations do not

1. For example, when the market for 8-track audio tapes was replaced by a market for cassette tapes, some small 8-track tape manufacturers declared bankruptcy. The market changed and inefficient firms were swept out of business, to be replaced by more efficient successors.

passively accept market dictates but instead actively work to transform their ties to other organizations that make up the market.

I argue that market models fail to shed much light on the bankruptcies of Manville, Continental, and Texaco because they lend too much credence to balance-sheet data. By accepting balance-sheet numbers as the only objective reality of the firm, market models can *logically* conclude that Manville, Texaco, Continental, A. H. Robins, and others declared bankruptcy because they had no other choice. But as you will see in the following pages, this view underestimates the extent to which companies and creditors make choices to shape the market data used to legitimate the claim to bankruptcy.

So it is not so much that market-based bankruptcy prediction models are wrong; they simply miss the most exciting part of the story. In the pages to follow, I spend as much analytical energy on what happened *before* the bankruptcy filing as I do on events subsequent to the filing. My central concerns include: How do liabilities and assets get defined prior to the bankruptcy petition? How do liabilities and assets become "official" liabilities and assets—that is, recognized by courts and government agencies as "real" liabilities and assets? What organizations have the power to influence these seemingly quantifiable, indisputable terms?

I begin with a brief tour through the history of bankruptcy law in chapter 1. My main objective here is to chart the broadening of bankruptcy as an arena in which to handle a larger array of social issues. I show how the Manville, Continental, and Texaco cases emerge from this historical widening of the bankruptcy forum and push the process another step further along. Specifically, I argue that legal changes have led to broader, more contentious definitions of seemingly technical, quantifiable concepts such as *debt, liability*, and *bankrupt*. These changes have given powerful institutions increased latitude in defining these terms to suit their interests.

In chapter 2, I discuss a variety of theories of the corporate bankruptcy process and show why they fail to uncover the strategic and political implications of bankruptcy. I focus on the weaknesses inherent in these theories and suggest we move away from the economic functionalism that has thus far dominated bankruptcy analysis. I borrow insights from a variety of fields to develop a framework for better understanding these cases.

Detailed case studies of the Manville, Continental, and Texaco bankruptcies occupy chapters 3, 4, and 5. In these chapters, I focus on the power of institutions to constrain and influence other institutions. I analyze the events leading up to the filing of a bankruptcy petition, as well as events following the filing. In each instance, I show how a Chapter 11 filing was *not* the only option available to the company, but rather was chosen from a constrained set of options. I detail the levers of power available to institutions both inside and outside the bankruptcy arena. Through these cases, it becomes clear that important social issues, with wide-ranging implications for the allocation of societal resources, are being decided by the powerful players in bankruptcy court.

In chapter 6, I address the larger theoretical and societal issues raised by my analysis and outline a new way to think about business bankruptcy. Rather than conceiving of the bankruptcy process as punishment, a neutral debt-collection device, or a market mechanism, I suggest that we view the bankruptcy forum as a political arena wherein large organizations attempt to use their power to avoid current financial burdens and shift future financial risk to more vulnerable groups. Conceptualizing bankruptcy in this way raises a set of important questions that have not been adequately addressed in the bankruptcy context: Does Chapter 11 act to facilitate debt collection in a neutral fashion? Does the Chapter 11 process actually fulfill its purported role of ensuring a healthy national economy by weeding out inefficient firms?

As more and more of our largest corporations declare bankruptcy for limited organizational purposes, we need to focus our attention more closely on the bankruptcy arena. Bankruptcy court has become the place where we decide how and when asbestos victims and women injured by the Dalkon Shield will be compensated, whether companies can eliminate unions, and how corporate giants settle takeover disputes. These questions were previously handled in other ways, such as through tort law,[2] the collective bargaining process, or by elected representatives in Congress. I hope this book provokes a debate over whether bankruptcy court is the best forum to find solutions to some of the most pressing social and political issues of our time.

2. A tort is a private or civil wrong, other than breach of contract, for which the court may provide a remedy in the form of damages.

1

Bankruptcy: From "Broken Bench" to "Fad of the Year"

All Bankrupts . . . ought to be hang'd. The pity of mankind has for ages run in a wrong channel, and has been diverted from poor Creditors . . . to scoundrel Debtors. . . . Trade will never reflourish in this Land till such a Law is establish'd.

—*Charles Lamb, letter to Bernard Barton,*
December 8, 1829

It may become almost "in" to say, "We're under court protection, are you?"

—*Unidentified official of*
Texas Air Corporation

The word *bankruptcy* comes from *banca rupta,* or broken bench, which referred to the Italian custom in medieval out-door markets of smashing the benches and stalls of mer-chants who did not pay their bills (see Tremain 1938). Jump ahead several centuries to January 20, 1986. On that day *Business Week* magazine listed Chapter 11 bankruptcy as one of the "top ten business trends" considered "in" that year. In the course of several centuries, we have somehow gone from "broken bench" to "fad of the year." Think about how dramatic this shift has been by juxtaposing the debtors' pris-ons of England and Frank Lorenzo's ranking as America's toughest manager because of his decision to put Continental and Eastern Air Lines into Chapter 11 bankruptcy.

Today, there are stock funds devoted entirely to investing in bankrupt companies, now called "bankruptcy plays" (*Business Week*, June 22, 1987, 162; *NYT*, September 10, 1986, D8). Bankruptcy lawyers are suddenly in great demand; "every major law firm is anxious to have a first-rate bankruptcy practitioner" (*Newsday*, April 19, 1987, 64). While our language has tried to keep up with the changing conception of the bankrupt, we are often forced into linguistic contortions to explain exactly what we mean by *bankrupt*. After Texaco's Chapter 11 filing, a supplier argued that the oil company somehow wasn't *really* bankrupt: "It's not like a company running out of money and can't afford to pay its bills" (*NYT*, April 13, 1987, A1). Some of our largest corporations are declaring bankruptcy and arguing that they aren't really broke.

The phenomena of corporations using bankruptcy as strategy did not appear out of thin air in the 1970s and 1980s. It is misleading to assume these cases are only owing to legal changes in the 1970s and 1980s. In this chapter, I suggest that the use of bankruptcy as a strategy is the result of several centuries of expanding the popular and legal conception of the bankrupt. There has been a continual widening of the availability of bankruptcy relief. This expansion has occurred through a series of important legal, political, economic, and social changes. In this chapter, I try to make sense out of how we got from here to there; that is, how we have gone from "broken bench" to "fad of the year."

THE EARLY ROOTS OF BANKRUPTCY LAW

Bankruptcy law can be traced as far back as 118 B.C. to a crude form of liquidation in Roman law. Under this law, the entire estate of a debtor was sold in one lump sale to a single buyer, who would then pay creditors a percentage of the debt owed to each. The debtor continued to be responsible for any remaining debt, and if it was not paid in fairly quick order, the debtor could be imprisoned, enslaved, exiled, or killed (Countryman 1976, 226).

The earliest bankruptcy statutes of Rome, England, and the Lombard cities (later to become the basis of the French bankruptcy system) applied only to individuals. In all of these early laws, bankruptcy was viewed as an *act* committed by an individual rather than as a person's economic *state of affairs*. That is why the earliest statutes used the word *fugitivi* (fugitive) more often than *banca-rotti* (bankrupt). These laws were aimed at fugitives: people who had committed an *act of bankruptcy* by fleeing to parts unknown without paying their bills (Tremain 1938, 192).

In medieval Europe, "flight to unknown parts" was the most common "act of bankruptcy" (Tremain 1927). Early bankruptcy statutes on the Continent contained as their central core elaborate rules to determine exactly when a debtor had withdrawn or fled from the marketplace and could thus legally be considered a "bankrupt" subject to bankruptcy law. In this sense, bankruptcy was a *social* and *moral* judgment rather than a purely economic definition based on a person's balance sheet. Someone was bankrupt when he or she violated the norms of the society and was judged a fugitive and a scoundrel, and thus a bankrupt.

Early English bankruptcy law was modeled on this tradition. However, "fleeing" was not as common in England as it was on the Continent. The reason for this was simple—the British debtor had a much more convenient way out of his debts and did not need to flee. The English common-law rule that "a man's house is his castle" prevented creditors from entering the debtor's house to garner money owed him, even if the creditor followed civil process and had a court order for the property. English debtors could simply lock their doors, close their shutters, and live in relative peace without paying debts. So in England this practice, called "keeping house," was a much more common act of bankruptcy than "fleeing" (Tremain 1927, 233).

If the English debtor disliked the idea of being shut up in his own house, he had yet another option to avoid his creditors—"sanctuary." Several large areas in England were deemed off limits to creditors attempting to wrest payment from debtors. Tremain (1927, 235) describes one such sanctuary in Westminster as being one-fourth of the city and the home to many debtors leading "extravagant lives thanks to the money from selling assets."

French merchants who had moved to England complained bitterly to Charles IX of France about the English practices of "keeping house" and "sanctuary." British merchants began one of the first lobbying efforts to use the law to improve creditors' ability to collect money owed them. This effort was eventually successful when, in 1623, English bankruptcy commissioners were given the right "to break open the bankrupt's house . . . and to seize upon and order the body, goods, chattels, ready money and other estate of such bankrupt as shall be thought by the commissioners necessary" (21 Jac. 1, c. 19, § 8 as quoted in Tremain 1927, 237).

Notice that although the *method* of avoiding creditors differed between England and the Continent, the underlying *principle* of bankruptcy remained the same: bankruptcy resulted from an action of the debtor that indicated he had withdrawn from the marketplace and violated the social customs of that particular community and the society at large. We can see this central principle of bankruptcy in the title of many of the early statutes. The House of Lords passed a bill titled "Merchants That Run Away with Other Men's Goods," and the first English bankruptcy law was a 1542 "Act against Such Persons as Do Make Bankrupt." Note that *bankrupt* was a *verb* to describe a socially unapproved action, not an *adjective* to describe a financial condition. As Tremain puts it, "Conduct, not financial embarrassment, was the gist of the offense" (Tremain 1938, 193).

Despite the availability to debtors of "flight," "keeping house," and "sanctuary," these were clearly not days of wine and roses for debtors, as anyone familiar with the history of the debtors' prisons of Europe can tell you. Debtors who were captured after committing an act of bankruptcy were often thrown in jail and held under quite unpleasant conditions.

A seventeenth-century court decision by Justice Sir Robert Hyde gives a sense of the attitude that the English common law held toward those who did not pay their creditors:

> If a man be taken in execution and lie in prison for debt, neither the plaintiff at whose suit he is arrested, nor the sheriff who took him, is bound to find him meat, drink, or clothes; but he must live on his own, or on the charity of others; and if no man will relieve him, let him die in the name of God. (Manby v. Scott, 1 Mod. 124, 132, 86 Eng. Rep. 781 [1659])

There was much more to the fear of bankruptcy, however, than simply the fear of jail. There was also the fear of community ostracism, often bordering on religious or moral damnation. A host of Victorian novels illustrate the widespread fear of bankruptcy among the populace and the moral stigma attached to being bankrupt that persisted through the nineteenth century (Weiss 1986). These novels give us a sense both of the way in which bankruptcy law operated in that era and of the moral taint attached to the bankrupt. For example, Charles Dickens's father ended up in debtors' prison, and this had such a profound influence on Dickens that the theme of bankruptcy turns up in two of his novels: *Dombey and Son* (1848) and *Little Dorrit* (1857). Similarly, Anthony Trollope's father sought sanctuary in Ostend, and Trollope included this event in *The Way We Live Now* (1875). Similar issues related to the fear of moral damnation attached to the bankrupt appear in Thackeray's *Vanity Fair* (1860), Charlotte Brontë's *Shirley* (1848), and George Eliot's *The Mill on the Floss* (1860) (Weiss 1986).

Clinging to the notion of bankruptcy as punishment and a formal act of bankruptcy as an offense to the community limited the ability of creditors to collect from debtors who were insolvent but had not fled or committed an act of bankruptcy. There was no provision in the laws of England or the Continent to handle the liquidation of these debtors' assets. This dismayed creditors seeking an effective way to liquidate the assets of all who owed them money, not just fugitives. Creditors were not only interested in the punishment of debtors, they also wanted their money back! The only method of relief for creditors seeking money from those who had not committed a bankruptcy act lay outside bankruptcy law in the realm of common law and involved a time-consuming process of proving a claim and then obtaining a writ to confiscate property.

Parliament came under pressure from the lending class to extend bankruptcy law to handle a wider variety of cases. But the popular conception of bankruptcy continued to require an action offensive to the community. To appease the lending class while at the same time handling the dissonance caused by breaking with the popular notion of bankruptcy as an action, Parliament created a legal fiction. In essence, it linguistically transformed non-actions into actions. Thus, a 1604 act defined "lying in prison for 6 months or more" as an act of bankruptcy by the debtor (1 Jac. 1, c. 15, § 2). As the scope of bankruptcy widened to handle more non-actions, the action fiction was retained in the law. A 1623 law added to the list of bankruptcy acts "being indebted for over 100 pounds, and not paying for 6 months" (21 Jac. 1, c. 19, § 2). Another non-action by the debtor—failure to pay—had been legally transformed into debtor action.

This legal fiction was stretched even further when laws passed in the eighteenth and nineteenth centuries broadened the definition of an act of bankruptcy to include *actions of other parties* as the actual actions of the debtor. Thus, an English act of 1914 contains this bizarre legal construction: "a debtor commits an act of bankruptcy . . . if execution has been levied by seizure of his goods under process" (4 & 5 Geo. 5, c. 59, § 1 [e]). In other words, the *debtor* committed an act of bankruptcy when a creditor took his property![1]

1. The first U.S. bankruptcy law, passed in 1800, would borrow the concept of an "act of bankruptcy," listing "departing from the state, keeping house, concealing oneself or disposing of property" as bankruptcy acts. The legal fiction of an act of bankruptcy was retained and linked with the insolvency requirement in the U.S. Bankruptcy Act of 1898: "A petition may be

Behind all of these linguistic and legal contortions was the broadening of the definition of a bankrupt to allow the court to handle cases in which a person was insolvent but had not committed a bankruptcy act. Thus we see in the roots of modern bankruptcy law the ever-widening scope of bankruptcy law and the changing definition of what it meant to be bankrupt. No longer was bankruptcy court solely a forum to punish debtors and liquidate the assets of those who had violated community norms. Instead, bankruptcy court gradually became an arena to adjudicate economic disputes and to collect debt, regardless of the intention or behavior of the debtor. Note the drastic change from the moral tone of the Victorian era in both the attitude toward the debtor and in the conception of the bankruptcy process:

> The true purpose of modern bankruptcy law is not to punish or deal with some conduct on the part of the debtor, but rather to administer a situation or condition whose economic incidents are of paramount concern. The important question which a modern bankruptcy law should ask is not, what and when did the debtor do something, but what is the debtor's actual condition at present. (Tremain 1938, 214)

Gradually courts began to employ an economic test to judge bankruptcy. The insolvency test, which measured whether the debtor's current assets were less than the amount of debt, began to take precedence over acts of bankruptcy as the main focus of bankruptcy law. "The matter of insolvency, which went practically unrecognized in the ancient law, acquired overshadowing importance" (Tremain 1938, 200). The core of bankruptcy law was gradually changing from punishing the debtor to dealing with the current financial condition of the debtor.

---

filed against a person who is insolvent and who has committed an act of bankruptcy within four months after the commission of such act."

BANKRUPTCY LAW IN THE UNITED STATES

Despite its appearance in the U.S. Constitution, the subject of bankruptcy was not a topic of great debate at the Constitutional Convention. In fact, bankruptcy was not mentioned until Charles Pickney of South Carolina suggested including the bankruptcy clause during the waning days of the convention (Warren 1935). With little debate, a clause was added to the Constitution giving Congress the power "to establish uniform laws on the subject of bankruptcy" (U.S. Constitution, Art. I, Sec. 8, clause 4).

Despite the specific mention in the Constitution of the federal government's right to establish bankruptcy laws, the United States was without such a national law for most of the eighteenth and nineteenth centuries, instead relying on state insolvency laws. In fact, the United States has had only five major bankruptcy acts. These were passed in 1800, 1841, 1867, 1898 (with important amendments in the 1938 Chandler Act), and 1978. Moreover, several of the laws had very short tenures: the 1800 Bankruptcy Act was repealed after just three years of operation, the 1841 act was repealed after a single year, and the 1867 act lasted a scant twelve years. So for most of the first two centuries after the adoption of the Constitution, creditors in the United States relied on state insolvency laws to collect money.

In the eighteenth and nineteenth centuries, several national economic crises brought new demands for a bankruptcy law to restore economic order to the country. Charles Warren, author of the authoritative study of the early history of bankruptcy in the United States, concluded that national debates on bankruptcy through 1935 had always occurred in response to nationwide economic upheaval: "From the beginning of our National Government every financial crisis and period of depression has been attended by the passage of stay-laws by state legislatures and by pressure on Congress for bankruptcy legislation" (Warren 1935, foreword).

Every U.S. bankruptcy law studied by Warren was the product of some major financial crisis or depression. In 1792, panic swept the country owing to wild speculation in government scrip. Thomas Jefferson warned against "the rage for getting rich in a day" in a letter to James Monroe (see Warren 1935, 7). This speculative bubble resulted in a major crash in 1793. Debate on establishing national bankruptcy laws immediately followed and increased through 1798.

Similarly, each successive economic crisis in the United States (1814, 1835, 1860, 1881, 1930s) was accompanied by calls for new bankruptcy laws. Each bankruptcy proposal provoked major political skirmishes, meeting with a variety of proponents and adversaries. Farmers and planters in the South tended to oppose the early bankruptcy laws, worrying that the laws were a means by which northern "money men" could press payment from farmers by threatening them with bankruptcy (Warren 1935). Commercial creditors in the North tended to favor a uniform system for collecting on debt and pushed for national legislation.

The first bankruptcy act in the United States was passed in 1800, but lasted less than three years before repeal. In the 33 months that the law was in effect, only 500 cases were heard in Pennsylvania, New York, Maryland, and the District of Columbia.[2] All parties complained of the difficulty of travel to federal courts. Creditors found that they only recovered a small percentage of the debt owed them, since most debtors were already in jail by the time formal bankruptcy proceedings got started.

At this time, bankruptcy still contained as its central core the notion of punishment. Debtors were not granted a discharge from debt, but continued to be liable for any money owed to creditors even after the liquidation of all of the debtor's assets. Thus, imprisonment for debt was a very common practice under state law until the mid nineteenth century.

2. These were the four areas with the highest number of cases.

According to court records collected in 1830 from Massachusetts, Maryland, New York, and Pennsylvania, three to five times as many persons were imprisoned for debt as for crime (Countryman 1976, 229).[3]

At this time, bankruptcy law only applied to individuals, and, prior to 1840, the only type of bankruptcy provided for in the law was involuntary bankruptcy, normally triggered by creditors. However, the 1841 law introduced a voluntary procedure for the first time. Many people thought "voluntary bankruptcy" was an oxymoron and wondered aloud why someone would ever *choose* bankruptcy. Joseph Trumbull of Connecticut reflected this sentiment in congressional debates on the voluntary provision: "Voluntary bankruptcy is a new term. Who ever heard such language before?" (Warren 1935, 72). This clear break with the old notions of bankruptcy as punishment caused dissonance for both legislators and the public, but it indicated that the bankruptcy arena was expanding.

The Bankruptcy Act of 1841 allowed for the discharge of debt, but creditors soon complained that too many individuals were granted a discharge, which they feared would encourage more and more debtors to declare bankruptcy. Of the 33,700 people who entered bankruptcy during the duration of the 1841 act, approximately 32,000 received some amount of discharge from debt (Countryman 1976, 229). Under intense pressure from creditors, the act was repealed just one year after passage.

A bill proposed in 1864 included for the first time a provision for the bankruptcy of companies. But the bill was defeated by the lobbying of a variety of commercial and trade groups who feared that a provision for business bankruptcy would give creditors tremendous power to force companies out of business. The chief proponents of the bill were north-

3. A wave of state reforms begun in the 1830s eventually led to the repeal of many of the state laws that imprisoned debtors.

ern creditors, who saw it as a way to wrest payment from firms that owed money.

The Bankruptcy Act of 1867 was the first law to include corporations. At creditors' behest, this act placed tighter restrictions on discharge from debt. Debts could only be discharged on the consent of a majority in number of creditors and a majority in the amount of claims held. Moreover, discharge was only allowed when assets were less than 30 percent of liabilities (Countryman 1976, 230).

These provisions severely curtailed the practice of discharge. During the eleven years that the 1867 act was on the books, an average of approximately 11,400 bankruptcy cases were heard each year, with about 400 cases involving a business debtor. In fewer than one-third of all cases were debtors granted any release from debt (Countryman 1976, 230). Despite these concessions, creditors ended up dissatisfied with even the restricted form of discharge and eventually managed to repeal the 1867 Bankruptcy Act in 1878.

By the time of the adoption of the Bankruptcy Act of 1898 (which was to last for eighty years), the concept of bankruptcy had fully evolved from an individual action offensive to the community and deserving punishment to an economic state of affairs (of individuals or companies) in which debts outweighed assets. Although there was still some stigma attached to the bankrupt, it had been greatly reduced since the days of the Lombard cities, when a debtor might lose an ear as punishment for an act of bankruptcy. In a speech on the Senate floor, David DeArmond of Missouri indicated how far bankruptcy law had come from the original notion of an act of bankruptcy: "The only just demand for any bankrupt bill is to be found in the sad state of honest but insolvent debtors. Such legislation should be designed not necessarily or primarily to distribute their estates . . . but to give them relief" (Warren 1935, 139).

The 1898 act, according to Warren, demonstrated "a rather general acceptance of the principle that a bankruptcy law

[was] required in the public interest of the nation" (Warren 1935, 144). Warren reflects the growing tendency to legitimate bankruptcy law as a way of resuscitating businesses in the name of the "national interest":

> Now, the chief interest of the Nation lies in the continuance of a man's business and the conservation of his property for the benefit of creditors and himself, and not in the sale and distribution of his assets among his creditors. . . . Forced sale of property and stoppage of a business in times of depression constitutes loss to the Nation at large, as well as to individual debtors and creditors. (Warren 1935, 144)

This goal of debtor rehabilitation gradually became elevated to stand alongside other norms reflected in bankruptcy, namely, the punishment of debtors and debt collection. As legislators and courts expanded bankruptcy law, it became clear that the law could be used as a political instrument to repair the economy: "Whatever may have been the anticipation of the framers, the fact is that the bankruptcy power has developed steadily, from being a regulation of traders for purely commercial purposes, into a national policy for relief, for creditors and debtors of all classes and for the restoration of business life, with debts adjusted or discharged" (Warren 1935, 8).

The idea of a "fresh start" for businesses, and specifically the goal of debtor rehabilitation, became formalized with the passage of the Chandler Act in 1938, which added Chapters X, XI, and XII to handle business bankruptcy.[4] Clearly the precipitating event for this legislation was the Great Depression, which led to the passage of emergency legislation to address the increase in business failures. Harvey Miller ob-

---

4. Before the bankruptcy amendments of 1933 and 1934 and the Chandler Act, corporate reorganization was accomplished through the use of an "equity receivership." Under this system, whoever put the company into receivership controlled the process. In most cases, this was the company, along with the cooperation of its largest bank creditor. This led to great dissatisfaction among other creditors, who often saw their interests trampled by a single creditor.

serves that the passage of the Chandler Act, the creation of the Reconstruction Finance Corporation, and other such entities "expressed the national policy that the best interests of the nation are promoted by affording commercial and industrial concerns the protection of bankruptcy law while they undergo financial and business rehabilitation" (Miller 1984, 1122).

But accompanying this growing interest in the goal of keeping businesses operating was also the recognition that bankruptcy could become an arena to handle larger social and economic problems, not simply an arena for debt collection. In the nineteenth century, William Fessenden of Maine foreshadowed this trend, suggesting that government had the right to act for the "public good," and to pursue social concerns, even to the extent of voiding contracts:

> The power of Government to pass laws affecting the obligation of contracts is derived from the nature of government itself . . . it is by no means difficult to imagine a condition of things in which the safety and well-being of the Nation would imperatively demand its exercise. Take the case, for example, in which a whole community becomes insolvent by some stupendous accident. . . . As a general rule, the obligation of contracts should be held inviolable. . . . But those rights and interests must yield to higher considerations of public policy. They must necessarily be made subservient to the good of the State. (Warren 1935, 158)

The financial crisis surrounding the Great Depression led to a sharp increase in bankruptcy filings. Total annual filings held relatively steady, ranging from a low of 13,000 to a high of 28,000 in the two decades following the 1898 act, but the number soared to 70,000 in 1932. The increase occurred in both personal and business filings. Legislators attempted to handle this sharp increase in business filings by passing the Chandler Act, which introduced three chapters designed to cover the range of business bankruptcies. Chapter X was created for the thoroughgoing reorganization of a company, typically involving the firm's complete recapitalization; Chapter

XI was intended to permit very simple compositions (debt arrangements) with unsecured creditors; and Chapter XII was designed to handle secured debt.

However, in the years following the passage of the Chandler Act, Chapter XI gradually became the most popular business chapter because of several advantages that debtor companies found when comparing it with the other chapters. For example, in most Chapter X cases, management was replaced by a court-appointed trustee, whereas in Chapter XI, management normally stayed in place. Under Chapter X, the reorganization plan also had to scale down the equity interest of management in the reorganized entity. Chapter X carried numerous cumbersome judicial procedures designed to ensure fairness to all parties in a complicated, thoroughgoing reorganization of a large firm. Obviously, managers looked for a way into Chapter XI rather than Chapter X in order to keep their jobs, equity interest, and control of the company.

But Chapter XI, because it was intended only for simple compositions, was a more flexible, free-wheeling chapter. Unlike Chapter X, Chapter XI did not require the appointment of a trustee to run the company and usually allowed management to stay in control. The Securities and Exchange Commission had a large role in Chapter X cases (to protect shareholder interests) but was much less involved in Chapter XI cases. Thus, Chapter XI cases usually involved less investigation of the company's finances and past business practices. Under Chapter XI, only the company could submit a reorganization plan, giving management a distinct advantage over other parties, particularly creditors. The debtor company often could delay filing a plan in order to remain under protection of the bankruptcy court.

The Chandler Act was far from precise in defining which chapter a particular business bankruptcy should follow. As a result, litigation often occurred on this issue. Businesses more and more chose Chapter XI over other chapters, despite the fact that the reorganization would deal with issues far more complex than ever envisioned by the authors of Chapter XI:

> It was inevitable that the existence of alternative schemes of rehabilitation, one of which leaves management firmly in control, and the other of which not only replaces management with an independent trustee, but investigates it, eliminates or scales down its equity holdings, would result in the filing of a Chapter XI, rather than a Chapter X, when any conceivable argument could be made for the propriety of that lesser form of relief. (Rosenberg 1975, 1151–52)

In the 1940s and 1950s, the SEC often challenged the propriety of Chapter XI filings and attempted to have many cases converted to Chapter X in order to "protect the public interest." The SEC argued that Chapter XI did not provide enough checks on management, and that management and commercial creditors often dominated the interests of shareholders. By the 1960s and 1970s, however, mainly owing to understaffing, the SEC gradually stopped challenging Chapter XI filings (King 1973, 430). This constituted the removal of a major barrier to the use of Chapter XI by large companies.

THE BANKRUPTCY REFORM ACT OF 1978

In 1970, Congress created the Commission on the Bankruptcy Laws of the United States and directed it "to study, analyze, evaluate and recommend changes" in the law in light of "technical, financial and commercial developments" that had occurred since the Chandler Act. The Brookings Institution was asked to do a study of the state of the bankruptcy process (see Stanley and Girth 1971).

The Brookings study revealed some of the reasons why Congress created the commission to alter bankruptcy law. First, the increase in the sheer number of bankruptcies was of great concern to commercial creditors. Since World War II, there had been a steady increase in the number of bankruptcies. Commercial creditors argued that this increase threatened the credit economy. David Stanley and Marjorie Girth reflect this sentiment in their report, saying: "A willingness to seek and extend credit is essential to the smooth functioning of the U.S. economy." In the thousands of pages of congressional testimony on proposed changes in the bankruptcy law, creditors expressed concern at the increase in bankruptcies and lamented the time-consuming process of collecting on debts through the bankruptcy process then in place.[5] Stanley and Girth conclude that bankruptcy was "a dreary, costly, slow, and unproductive process" (1971, 197). Bankruptcy law was defended as an instrument that, if properly designed, could "ensure a smooth national economy."

Although the Brookings study reported a rise in both personal and business bankruptcies, it was really the personal bankruptcy rate that had soared dramatically. Business bankruptcies had increased, but at a much more gradual pace. Even though Stanley and Girth (1971) stated that business bankruptcies had increased only gradually over the past two decades, many bankruptcy experts and commercial creditors used this opportunity to revamp business bankruptcy law as well as personal bankruptcy law.

Certainly there were areas in business bankruptcy law that interest groups were eager to alter. Both creditors and debtors had complained about the existence of three different bankruptcy chapters (X, XI, and XII) to handle business cases. The differences between the three chapters had gradually blurred since their introduction in the Chandler Act in 1938, occasionally leading to costly litigation about which chapter a case properly belonged under. This litigation was clearly a reflection of the fact that each chapter afforded relative advantages and disadvantages to interests in a given case. Creditors often used the threat of litigating a push to-

5. See hearing documents from the House Judiciary Committee, Subcommittee on Civil and Constitutional Rights, and the Senate Subcommittee on Improvements of Judicial Machinery, summaries in *U.S. Code Cong. & Ad. News* 1978a, b.

ward Chapter X to gain concessions from a debtor company. Businesses continued to choose Chapter XI, since it allowed management to stay in charge of the company.

The Bankruptcy Commission expressed great concern that Chapter XI was increasingly being used improperly by large companies. Chapter XI was created for small, privately owned businesses and therefore had more informal procedures than Chapter X, but it was being used by companies with huge levels of debt and very complex financial structures. Creditors complained that they had little control over management during a Chapter XI process and pressed for increased authority for the creditors' committees.

Another oft-heard complaint during the hearings centered on the representativeness of the creditors' committee. A creditors' committee was set up in Chapter XI cases to represent the interests of all creditors. But often the creditors' committee was weighted in favor of a single class of creditors. The interests of trade creditors (suppliers) and commercial lenders (banks), for example, might differ. Members of the creditors' committee were elected by votes apportioned according to the number of creditors and the amount owed to each creditor. As a result, "more often than not the committee [was] dominated by institutional creditors at the expense of individuals" (Rosenberg 1975, 1164).

Ironically, the move to revamp the bankruptcy code was born out of the mistaken (or at least exaggerated) concern that bankruptcy rates were rising—which was not really true in the case of business bankruptcy. The legal changes that resulted from these debates ended up causing the very problem that the new code was supposed to address. Business bankruptcy filings soared by 150 percent between 1978 and 1987, including a 600 percent increase in Chapter 11 filings. It is difficult, of course, to determine what portion of this increase was owing solely to legal changes and what part to the economic recession during those years. However, one careful economic analysis suggested that approximately 19 percent of business filings between 1978 and 1983 were owing directly to the broadening of the bankruptcy law (Marsh and Cheng 1985). Thus, in regard to the changes in the 1978 code, it would not be far off the mark to conclude that the "solution" ended up causing the problem, which had never really been there to begin with.

Perhaps the most important reason for the changes in business bankruptcy law was that Congress and the Bankruptcy Commission looked to continue the trend of increasing the scope of problems handled under bankruptcy law. According to the framers of the legislation eventually passed in 1978, "both substantively and administratively, the bankruptcy system was straining on all sides to handle situations that the framers of the current law never dreamed would arise" (*U.S. Code Cong. & Ad. News* 1978b, 5965). The complaint was often made at the congressional hearings (by both corporations and lenders) that by the time a company was able to seek reorganization under bankruptcy, it was often beyond salvation. In hope of giving firms a better chance of surviving, a number of bankruptcy experts suggested broadening the conditions under which a firm could seek to reorganize. The logic behind this position was that the earlier a firm could take advantage of things like an automatic stay on debt payments, the greater the chance of gaining a plan of reorganization that would allow the firm to survive. In this, we see the continued elevation of the goal of debtor rehabilitation over the goal of survival of the fittest.

The process of revamping the nation's bankruptcy code was a contentious one to say the least. Frank Kennedy, executive director of the Bankruptcy Commission, wrote that "practically every improvement favored by a particular group was strongly opposed by others" (Kennedy 1980, 672). After nearly a decade of debate, the 95th Congress passed a comprehensive new bankruptcy law, and President Jimmy Carter signed the bill on November 6, 1978. The Bankruptcy Act of 1978 (Pub. L. No. 95–598, 92 Stat. 2549) was only the fifth major federal bankruptcy law passed in U.S. history. As such, it was met with great anticipation and a wealth of analysis as interested parties tried to assess the impact of the legal changes.

One of the most important changes in the new Bankruptcy Code was the broadening of the definition of a claim. A "claim," of course, is one of the basic building blocks of any declaration of bankruptcy. If the total of all "claims" overwhelms assets, then the company is deemed insolvent. The new code defined a claim in astonishingly broad legal language as "any right to payment, whether or not reduced to judgment, liquidated, unliquidated, fixed, contingent, matured, unmatured, disputed, undisputed, legal, equitable, secured, or unsecured" (*U.S. Code Cong. & Ad. News* 1978a, 5808).

While the new definition of a claim was judged "a significant departure from present law" (*U.S. Code Cong. & Ad. News* 1978a, 5807), when viewed in historical context, this is simply another example of the broadening of the bankruptcy arena. Congress clearly expressed this intention in its report on the bill: "By this broadest possible definition . . . the bill contemplates that all legal obligations of the debtor, no matter how remote or contingent, will be able to be dealt with in the bankruptcy case. It permits the broadest possible relief in the bankruptcy court" (ibid., 5808).

This broad definition of a claim would enable the bankruptcy court to consider future claims, not yet matured or reduced to judgment. Future tort liabilities not yet even known, for example, could be handled in the bankruptcy arena. The concept of "equity insolvency" (where future liabilities would outweigh future assets) was elevated to stand alongside "balance-sheet insolvency" (when current liabilities outweigh current debt).

However, there were numerous problems inherent in trying to estimate *future* assets and liabilities. Both could be open to widely competing interpretations by various interests in a bankruptcy case. Congress, however, tried to downplay this problem with a bit of wishful thinking: "The equity insolvency test has been in equity jurisprudence for hundreds of years and though it is new in the bankruptcy context, the bankruptcy courts should have no difficulty in applying it" (*U.S. Code Cong. & Ad. News* 1978a, 5820). However, one bankruptcy judge indicated that this application might not be as straightforward as Congress hoped, calling the actual process "at best a ballpark guess" (Rosenberg 1975, 1186).

Under the new law, Chapters X, XI, and XII were consolidated into a single Chapter 11.[6] Now only two chapters were available to businesses: Chapter 11 for reorganization and Chapter 7 for liquidation. Perhaps the most significant change in Chapter 11 involved the appointment of a trustee to oversee the company during the reorganization process. Under the new law, current management is automatically authorized to continue in control of the filing company unless there is "a showing that a trustee is necessary to preserve the property of the estate or to prevent loss to the estate" (*U.S. Code Cong. & Ad. News* 1978a, 5820). Under old Chapter X, this assumption was not made and current management had to prove to the court that it should remain in control of the company. Thus, the new code made it more likely that current management would continue in place during the bankruptcy process. Obviously, this made declaring bankruptcy more appealing to managers worried about their jobs.

The new law also reduced the role of the bankruptcy judge and elevated the role of the creditors' committee. Under old Chapter X, for example, the bankruptcy court performed a valuation of the business. Now, this task would be left to negotiation between the debtor and its creditors. The law states only that the valuation must fall somewhere between the liquidation value of the company (selling off the various parts of the company) and its "going-concern value" (what the company is worth kept together).

6. I am following the legal convention of using Roman numerals for chapters under the 1898 Bankruptcy Act and Arabic numerals for chapters under the 1978 Bankruptcy Reform Act.

Drafters of the new bankruptcy code admitted that in the past, valuation was far from a scientific practice:

> Though valuation is theoretically a precise method of determining creditors' and shareholders' rights in a business, more often the uncertainty of predicting the future, [means] valuation is a method of fudging a result that will support the plan that has been proposed ... such a valuation is usually "a guess compounded by an estimate." (*U.S. Code Cong. & Ad. News* 1978b, 6181)

But removing the court from this valuation process and leaving it to negotiation between creditors and the debtor did nothing to alter the nature of valuation as "a guess compounded by an estimate" and "usually a fudging of a result to support a proposed plan." Indeed, reducing the court's authority in this process promised to give managers and commercial creditors even more power to fashion the "fudged result."

With the restriction of the court's involvement in overseeing the debtor's actions, the creditors' committee became even more important: "The importance of the committee cannot be overstated. The court's removal from administrative involvement in the case places upon the committee ... the burden of monitoring the debtor's operations" (Moller and Foltz 1980, 907).

The creditors' committee was made responsible for assisting in determining whether the business should stay in operation, whether the court should appoint a trustee to oversee the business, and whether to conduct an investigation into the financial affairs of the debtor. Under the new law, the creditors' committee normally met without the bankruptcy judge. Two legal theorists sum up the net results of the changes: "The committees appointed under the [new] Code provisions will exercise a great deal more power and control than was ever possible for a committee under old Chapter XI" (Moller and Foltz 1980, 914).

An article in the *Banking Law Journal* (Rome 1979, 416–17) provided this advice for the commercial lender in dealing with the new bankruptcy law. Note that the article predicted the use of bankruptcy as strategy:

> Creditors' committees [will have] increased power. Since the seven largest creditors holding unsecured claims will ordinarily . . . be appointed to the creditors' committee in a Chapter 11, active participation by bank lenders should be seriously considered. . . . The Bankruptcy Act of 1978 should cause bank lenders to readjust attitudes and practices to the realities of bankruptcy filings against *solvent* companies . . . [and] the likelihood in a Chapter 11 reorganization of intense and significant negotiation and bargaining. (emphasis mine)

Despite this increased power of the creditors' committee, the new law did little about the problem of the representativeness of the committee. In fact, under the new code, the committee was normally to be made up of the seven largest creditors. More often than not, the committee was dominated by institutional creditors at the expense of smaller creditors (Rosenberg 1975, 1164).

Under the new Chapter 11, lenders could file their own reorganization plan after the debtor's period of exclusivity (120 days) elapsed and could file a competing plan after 180 days. This gave creditors a significant threat to use against the debtor: if the company's reorganization plan was not filed quickly, or was not to the liking of creditors, a creditor could file a competing plan of reorganization.

Robert Rosenberg (1975, 1163) has argued that rather than acting as a check upon the debtor, creditors often assume the role of aiding management against other parties to the case (e.g., shareholders, employees): "Conceived of as a check upon the powers and control of the debtor-in-possession, and to some extent as a substitute for an independent trustee, in far too many cases, the creditors' committee becomes a tool of management or of its agents, or an instrument of repression for one creditor or class of creditors to dominate the others."

Allowing consideration of future claims not yet known makes definitions of *claim, insolvent, asset, debt,* and *bankrupt* more hazy and open to competing interpretations. These changes gave organizations the opportunity to bring power to bear in defining these terms to meet their interests. We might expect, then, that the valuation process would be fought over even less clear definitions of assets and liabilities, since the fight would now center on *future* assets and liabilities.

Clearly, then, legal changes opened the door a bit wider for the increased use of bankruptcy as a strategy. The overhaul of the nation's bankruptcy code led attorneys to rethink the role of corporate bankruptcy, and many legal experts became more interested in the area as a result of this opportunity. For the first time, the subject of bankruptcy became a "sexy" legal specialty, and many of the major law firms sought to add bankruptcy practitioners. Skadden, Arps, New York's largest law firm, had no lawyers working on bankruptcy in 1979, but by 1987 the firm had twenty-two attorneys assigned to bankruptcy cases. Skadden, Arps played a leading role in developing novel legal arguments, handling the reorganizations of both Manville and A. H. Robins. Weil, Gotshal, an important player in the Texaco case, had a bankruptcy department numbering some sixty lawyers in 1987, close to 15 percent of the total firm (*Newsday*, April 19, 1987, 64).

Business bankruptcy cases began to mean big money for law firms. Leading attorneys earned fees as high as $300 per hour. Previously granted "no respect," business bankruptcy lawyers found themselves thrust into the limelight. As the *Wall Street Journal* reported at the time, "Bankruptcy lawyers are no longer the Rodney Dangerfields of corporate law" (July 9, 1987, 31).

Legal practitioners, drawn to the area, began to see opportunities for using Chapter 11 in new ways—namely, as financial strategy—just as several firms were searching for solutions to major business crises. Bankruptcy lawyers became involved in thinking, not just about assets and debts, but about entire financial and corporate strategies, with Chapter 11 filings as the centerpiece of the strategy.

CONCLUSION

The stigma attached to a bankrupt corporation has declined dramatically over the past two centuries. As economists might put it, the decrease in stigma lowered the cost to companies of declaring bankruptcy. By the 1980s, bankruptcy had completely shed its previous use as a punishment for violation of the social and moral order. As I have outlined above, a host of important legal changes accompanied and encouraged this reduction in stigma. Voluntary bankruptcy, discharge from debt, debt moratoria, and Chapter 11 reorganization for corporations have all been added to a law that was initially designed to punish violators of marketplace norms. The emergence of bankruptcy as a strategy thus required both legal changes and a change in the social conception of what it means to be bankrupt. As you will see in the pages that follow, the Chapter 11 filings of Manville, Continental Airlines, and Texaco illustrate how bankruptcy has become a corporate strategy.

Journalists have sometimes recognized the use of bankruptcy as a strategy, but they often imply that these cases are a subversion of the true nature of bankruptcy law. I see these bankruptcies, however, as part of the historical trend of widening the availability of bankruptcy protection. The fundamental legal changes in 1978 were another step in this process. Broadening the definition of a claim made bankruptcy even less of a technical, economic matter (i.e., an economic ratio between debts and assets) and has given commercial creditors and corporate management greater leeway in constructing the definition of *bankrupt*.

Perhaps not surprisingly, the adoption of each new bankruptcy law has been accompanied by fighting between a variety of interests trying to shape the law in their favor. These interests have changed over time (merchants and traders versus farmers; northern interests versus southern interests; commercial creditors versus corporations; labor versus corporations). But in reviewing the history of bankruptcy legislation, one thing is clear—bankruptcy law is a political instrument that can elevate one group's interests at the expense of those of other groups.[7]

The justification for having a bankruptcy law is, however, that it is in the "national interest," rather than in the interest of any one group at the expense of others. The "national interest" is said to be served because the process ensures systemwide efficiency. As I have suggested, though, there is a tension between allowing creative destruction (forcing inefficient firms out of business) on the one hand and using bankruptcy law to restore "economic order" during times of crisis by rehabilitating debtors and keeping businesses together on the other hand. Much of bankruptcy theory ignores the historical reality that bankruptcy has been used as a political instrument.

After the Bankruptcy Reform Act of 1978, bankruptcy court would soon become a forum in which to solve our asbestos health crisis, to put a value on death from asbestos, to shape the contours of the collective bargaining process between labor and management, and to determine the rules of the corporate takeover game. As I argue in the next chapter, social scientists and legal theorists have not considered the strategic and political implications of the bankruptcy

7. Creditors, more than any other group, have been active in shaping bankruptcy law. For lenders, bankruptcy acts as an outer limit to financial risk. It has gone largely unrecognized in the literature on the separation of ownership and day-to-day control of the modern corporation that bankruptcy has contributed to this separation by placing an outer limit on lenders' risk. Owners of capital might have been less willing to extend capital without the protection of bankruptcy law. At the very least, a lack of bankruptcy laws might increase the cost of capital.

process. Instead, these theorists continue to treat bankruptcy as an adverse financial condition that managers begrudgingly accept when undisputed balance-sheet figures and market forces leave them with no other option. You will see in the following chapter that bankruptcy law is often portrayed in these theories as a neutral market mechanism rather than a political instrument. It is to this view of bankruptcy in academic, legal, and business literature that I now turn.

2

Theories of Corporate Bankruptcy

> Business bankruptcies usually result from a
> combination of poor business management and
> unfavorable market conditions.
> —*David Stanley and Marjorie Girth,*
> Bankruptcy: Problem, Process, Reform

> Business failure, including the legal procedures of
> corporate bankruptcy liquidation and reorganization,
> is a sobering economic reality reflecting the uniqueness
> of the American way of corporate death.
> —*Edward Altman,* Corporate Financial
> Distress: A Complete Guide to Predicting,
> Avoiding and Dealing with Bankruptcy

The very idea of bankruptcy as strategy challenges not only our commonsense notion of bankruptcy as a place to avoid but also a host of theoretical approaches to the study of business bankruptcy that have always underplayed the strategic nature of the process. In this chapter, I discuss a variety of theories of corporate bankruptcy and propose a sociological perspective that recognizes the strategic and political implications of business bankruptcy.

To demonstrate how deeply we accept the idea of bankruptcy as a bad place, consider for a moment Dun & Bradstreet's yearly listing of business failures in the United States, which classifies bankruptcies by presumed cause.

"Experience factors," such as management incompetence, lack of line experience, and unbalanced experience, and "economic factors," such as low profits, high interest rates, loss of market, and no consumer spending, were said to account for 92 percent of the business failures in 1987, 89.1 percent of failures in 1986, and 86.3 percent in 1985 (Dun & Bradstreet 1985; 1986).[1] The Dun & Bradstreet view is not very different from a Commerce Department study done in 1932, which concluded that the major causes of business bankruptcies were inefficient management, unwise use and extension of credit, adverse domestic and personal factors, and dishonesty and fraud (see Sadd and Williams 1932; see also Dewing 1926).

Embedded in Dun & Bradstreet's classification, the Commerce Department and Brookings Institution studies, and most bankruptcy theories is the view that bad managers and bad times cause bankruptcy (Delaney 1989a). But this "explanation" of the causes of bankruptcy is like saying that 90 percent of divorces are due to incompatibility. It fails to delve below surface explanations. In fact, it sometimes borders on tautological, since bad management is only looked for in firms that have failed and there is no effort to compare management of a bankrupt firm with a non-bankrupt firm. It is simply assumed that if the firm went bankrupt, it *must* have had bad management. But as I demonstrated in chapter 1, changes in the law have opened up the bankruptcy arena. I shall demonstrate in the case studies of Manville, Continental Airlines, and Texaco that follow that the behavior of corporations and commercial creditors have made bankruptcy a *proactive* strategy.

1. The remaining 10 percent or so of bankruptcies fall into such categories as "lack of sales," "heavy operating expenses," and "management neglect." Interestingly, Dun & Bradstreet recently changed its category "expense causes" to "finance causes." This new category includes "burdensome institutional debt," "heavy operating expenses," and "insufficient capital." While more closely approaching a description of reality, this categorization continues to assume that all bankruptcies are reactions rather than actions.

ECONOMIC THEORIES OF BUSINESS BANKRUPTCY

Economists have generated the majority of work among so-cial scientists on business bankruptcy. But even economists have not spent much theoretical energy on the issue of bank-ruptcy. Edward Altman, the leading figure in the field, has lamented his profession's lack of interest in the topic. "The subject of corporate bankruptcy has been relegated to a de-scriptive chapter or two invariably found at the end of a basic business finance textbook," he observes (Altman 1971, xix). I think the slighting of bankruptcy in economic litera-ture is partly because it has been treated as unproblematic for equilibrium models, which simply assume that bank-ruptcy is a technical, financial state in which a firm's debts outweigh its assets. According to microeconomic models, a firm in this position will be forced out of business and anoth-er, more efficient successor will simply take up the market niche left by the exiting firm. Therefore, these models as-sume that more productive firms are constantly replacing less productive firms, thereby leading to increased system-wide efficiency and an overall market composed of firms producing at the minimum average cost given existing tech-nology (Alchian 1953; Day 1975; Hirschman 1970; Aldrich 1979; Hannan and Freeman 1977).

This lack of attention to the corporate bankruptcy process is surprising and troubling. I think microeconomists *should* be concerned with the operation of corporate bankruptcy, since their theories center on the exit of firms from the mar-ket. Chapter 11 bankruptcy is a major means by which we decide which firms are dissolved and which are reorganized and permitted to continue in business. The bankruptcy pro-cess, then, is a significant part of the "natural selection" component of any "survival of the fittest" model, and we must ask whether it works properly to allow efficient firms to stay in business while sweeping away inefficient firms.

In the 1980s, it was not unusual for 50,000 businesses to declare bankruptcy in a given year. Generally, a third of these firms sought to reorganize. If we find that the process of deciding which firms are allowed to reorganize and which are liquidated is influenced by organizational power as much as by economic imperatives, or, alternately, that the bankruptcy court is simply unable to make a valid distinction between an "efficient" and an "inefficient" firm, a major tenet of "survival of the fittest" models would be called into question.

Macroeconomists, unlike microeconomists, have paid a good deal of attention to corporate bankruptcy and have produced the vast majority of the social science literature on the topic. Altman (1971; 1983) investigated the relationship between business failure and other aggregate macroeconomic phenomena, developing a multivariate model to predict national levels of bankruptcies. A host of analysts operating in this tradition have focused on the task of predicting the level of firm failure by exploring the link between the individual firm's balance sheet and a series of large-scale cyclical market factors in the overall economy (see also Beaver 1968; Gordon 1971; Hutchinson et al. 1938; Johnson 1970; Meyer and Pifer 1970).

This focus is quite useful if your aim is to predict overall levels of business bankruptcies nationwide, and indeed Altman and others provide sophisticated models for just this purpose. But the conclusions drawn from this work—that bankruptcy is caused, and can be also be explained, by internal balance-sheet data and cyclical, large-scale macroeconomic factors—are not very different from the Dun & Bradstreet and Commerce Department views (Altman 1971, 55). "The overwhelming cause of individual firm failures is managerial incompetence," Altman concluded (1983, 40).

There are several problems with the market-model perspective. First, these analysts take balance-sheet data for granted as the only portrayal of the firm's financial state. In the case studies to follow, we shall see that this is a dangerous assumption. Analysis of balance-sheet data provided with a Chapter 11 filing often leads to the conclusion that managers had no alternative other than a bankruptcy filing. But where do these balance-sheet numbers come from? I shall demonstrate in the cases that follow that much of what winds up on a firm's balance sheet is actually constructed by various institutional actors in the firm's network. We must thus study the power and influence of institutional actors to shape the "bottom line," and hence the crisis leading to bankruptcy.

Second, these analysts alternately narrow their focus to numbers on the company's balance sheet (e.g., debt-to-equity ratios, debt-to-asset ratios, cash-flow indicators) and then widen their vision to national market factors (e.g., national interest rate, stage in the business cycle). The territory in between is left unexplored. These models thus tend to ignore the immediate socioeconomic milieu of the firm: its relationship with creditors, suppliers, insurers, the government, courts, and other organizations within its immediate network. This produces a perspective that shares the fundamental assumption of the managerialist view of corporate action in general; that is, that bankruptcy is mainly an internal decision by management, and that links between firms and markets are only through tenuous, large-scale market ties, such as the national interest rate, general consumer demand, and the like. The upshot is a view of the company as atomistic.

A further problem arises because of the tendency in many of these models to subsume Chapter 11 bankruptcy under the general heading of business failure—perhaps the most extreme example of treating bankruptcy as an anathema to "good business," rather than as a strategy. Bankruptcy is interpreted as just one permutation of a larger category that includes such diverse phenomena as the voluntary exit of a firm from the market, foreclosure or attachment, voluntary compromise with creditors, and "straight bankruptcy" (Chapter 7 dissolution). Lumping together Chapter 11 bankruptcy and the voluntary closing of a firm indicates just how far we have come in accepting the view of bankruptcy as a last resort and part of the larger phenomenon of "business failure."

The way in which law affects the very definition of "bankrupt," as well as the definition of "rational action," is also left unquestioned by market models. In the case studies that follow, we shall see, however, that changes made to the U.S. Bankruptcy Code in 1978 were crucial to the definition of such seemingly empirical terms as *debt, liability, asset,* and *insolvent.* As a result of legal changes, actions considered "economically rational" after 1978 (i.e., a Chapter 11 bankruptcy filing) might not have been seriously contemplated before 1978. Changes in the legal context of business crisis and the role of the state in fashioning these legal changes thus demand more analysis than is provided in models that include Chapter 11 under the general category "business failure" and take the legal context for granted.

In sum, the dominant economic portrait of business bankruptcy is based on problematic assumptions. First, bankruptcy is treated as an economic state that a firm finds itself in when its liabilities outweigh its assets, and is viewed as organizational response or adaptation. Based on this view, bankruptcy is "predicted" through the ratios of debt to equity and cash flow to debt, and other such indicators, combined with large-scale macroeconomic indicators such as national interest rates and stage in the business cycle. Balance-sheet indicators are assumed to be empirically definable, mathematically measurable, and not subject to dispute, while nationwide macroeconomic factors are assumed to affect all firms equally. The conclusion drawn from this is that bankruptcy is mainly "caused" by problems internal to the firm or endemic to the national marketplace.

LEGAL THEORIES OF BUSINESS BANKRUPTCY

Recently, the legal literature on bankruptcy has been strongly influenced by what is called "the law and economics movement." This school, more than any other legal tradition, has attempted to construct a general theory of bankruptcy (Jackson 1986). This movement has borrowed extensively from the economic tradition discussed above, and its theory of bankruptcy therefore suffers from some of the same shortcomings. Law-and-economics theory believes that bankruptcy law is not, and should not be, concerned with business rehabilitation. Instead, the court should only be concerned with what is most efficient for the overall economy. Thus, bankruptcy law, if designed properly, must encourage creditors and debtors to choose bankruptcy at the time when it maximizes the money available to creditors as a group. Moreover, the court chooses between reorganization and liquidation based on whether the firm is worth more kept operating (reorganized) or sold off (liquidated) (Baird 1986). Thus, much of the legal literature on bankruptcy focuses on designing bankruptcy procedures that impel firms and their creditors to "choose" bankruptcy at the most efficient time (Posner 1972; Weistart 1977; Weston 1977; Jackson 1986; Baird 1987b).

According to the law-and-economics theory, bankruptcy law need not worry about questions of the fairness of allocation of proceeds among creditors, because these questions are handled outside of bankruptcy law. In other words, the rights of each party in a bankruptcy case are established *prior* to the bankruptcy filing and the bankruptcy court need only enforce pre-petition rights. So, for example, commercial banks often bargain for the priority of their claims by adding covenants to loans made to corporations that state that no other loan to the company can take precedence in the event of bankruptcy. The bank would then be paid before unsecured parties should the company declare bankruptcy. Bankruptcy law need not be concerned with this, since it falls outside of a strict interpretation of the scope of bankruptcy law.

But, the ploy of pushing all questions about rights outside of the bankruptcy arena simply skirts pressing political and sociological questions. What power do various parties have to bargain for superior positions before and in bankruptcy? How do they get this power? Do a commercial bank and an asbestos victim have equal bargaining power to gain precedence?

But even taken on its own grounds, there are several problems with the law-and-economics approach. First, these studies almost without exception deduce how rational businesses *would* behave, given existing legal rules, rather than analyzing how organizations *actually* behave in bankruptcy. Few empirical studies exist to test whether firms behave as these theorists predict. Even within the deductive framework of law-and-economics theory, it is far from clear that bankruptcy rules trigger the efficient outcomes the theory predicts. White (1989) demonstrates that many bankruptcy rules may actually encourage firms and creditors to choose options maximally advantageous to their *individual* interests but that do not maximize the money available to creditors as a group.

Additionally, law-and-economics theory assumes full and undeviatingly rational behavior on the part of managers and organizations. But a wealth of literature has demonstrated that organizations exist in a world of "bounded" or limited rationality (Simon 1976; March and Simon 1958; Perrow 1986). In the real world, managers operate with limited knowledge, and people in organizations can pursue a variety of conflicting goals, some of which may be irrational from a strictly economic point of view. Since managers of firms may experience extreme pressure from creditors during bankruptcy, it seems folly to assume undeviating rationality. One study that did explore managerial behavior during bankruptcy concluded that managers often acted in ways opposite from doctrinal predictions (Nelson 1981). There is thus evidence that the doctrinal view needs to be tested by analyzing actual organizational behavior.

Legal theorists outside of the law-and-economics tradition often argue that a general theory of bankruptcy is impossible, since bankruptcy law develops through case law (Carlson 1987). Since various judges in numerous jurisdictions across the country and across time make case decisions, bankruptcy law develops in fits and starts, moving in various directions, and thus evades general theorizing.

While eschewing a general bankruptcy theory, most legal writers point to general principles inherent in the law that ensure fairness in bankruptcy court. Two major bankruptcy rules are important in this regard: absolute priority and temporal equality. According to absolute priority, each claim against the debtor is assigned a priority level. For example, secured creditors (those who negotiated for collateral to secure their claims) are on a top-priority level and are paid first (after government claims and taxes, of course). This priority level is paid in full before the next level (unsecured creditors) receives anything. If there is not enough money to pay all on the same level in full, each receives a pro rata share of money owed according to the principle of temporal equality. If money is left over after paying all parties on the top level in full, the next level, unsecured creditors, is then paid.[2] Only after both secured and unsecured creditors are paid in full on their claims do shareholders receive any of the firm's value.

These legal rules are supposed to ensure that all on the same level are treated fairly, and the role of the bankruptcy judge, according to legal-doctrinal approaches, is to "balance the equities" of all parties. But what does this mean? How do you balance the equities of parties with vastly different interests? It seems to mean in practice that the bank-

2. The statuses of "secured" and "unsecured" depend on whether the creditors' claims are secured by actual collateral. The status of a "secured" creditor is subject to bargaining between the firm and the creditor. Often, commercial banks will include covenants in loans that prevent the firm from incurring any secured debt that threatens their status. Thus, organizational power is instrumental in the defining of priority levels, which in turn are crucial in determining the amount of payment. A large commercial bank often bargains for secured status, while asbestos victims are assigned to unsecured status.

ruptcy judge makes a decision based on his or her view of the rights of various parties. But we do not really know if some institutions tend to win or lose in bankruptcy court. Are some parties more likely to have their interests protected by the court? Are there pressures on bankruptcy judges to keep companies operating and to make sure bank creditors get paid? We lack the empirical data, whether of the large-scale-survey or the case-study variety, to know whether equities really are balanced in bankruptcy court.

In the small collection of cases I shall analyze, it is clear that these rules are not implemented. In most cases, reorganization plans are subject to extensive negotiation, and a great deal of bargaining over payoff occurs. One priority level, for example, may agree to take less and give another priority level something in order to gain their endorsement of the plan. Clearly, then, power enters into the bargaining over payoff. Yet we have not really studied the role of power in the bankruptcy arena.

Many legal analysts also assume that assets and liabilities are definable beyond dispute, and that parties cannot use their power and influence to shape assets and liabilities to suit their interests. Legal analysts and policymakers have not given enough attention to the bargaining that occurs before and during the bankruptcy process, instead assuming that all parties bargain on an equal footing. They have not, for example, looked at how large, powerful organizations might use their power and influence to affect the timing of a bankruptcy filing, their own status in terms of priority level, the bargaining over the reorganization plan, or the final outcome. We know that commercial creditors control loan capital that is needed by almost all firms after their emergence from Chapter 11. How this leverage might be turned into actual gains in bargaining over payoff remains a pressing sociological and legal question. Do asbestos victims and labor unions actually stand on an equal footing with a large commercial bank? If not, bankruptcy may not act as a neutral debt-collection device that treats all those with a claim against the debtor fairly.

JOURNALISTIC ACCOUNTS OF BANKRUPTCY

Whereas scholarly theories from a variety of disciplines have underplayed the strategic nature of bankruptcy, a few journalistic accounts of major Chapter 11 cases have hinted at the use of bankruptcy as a strategy (Brown 1988; *Business Week*, April 29, 1985, 31; Vartan 1986). In the popular and business press, several articles have appeared criticizing or praising managers of some of the largest bankrupt firms for using bankruptcy as strategy. Critics have argued that management chose bankruptcy to avoid corporate responsibilities, while advocates have asserted that management chose bankruptcy to protect shareholders and employees.

Although these accounts recognize that strategy was involved, they are unable fully to explicate either the nature of this strategy or the variety of institutional players involved in shaping bankruptcy strategy. Interestingly, both critics *and* supporters shared the view that management alone was *choosing* Chapter 11 bankruptcy. Thus, those writers that did recognize the strategic implications of Chapter 11 overplayed the power of management and underplayed the role of other organizations. By and large, these views missed the role of auditors, bond-rating agencies, commercial banks, shareholders, insurance companies, and other actors that played crucial parts in shaping these bankruptcies. An interorganizational analysis promises to yield a richer understanding of how strategy is shaped and the sources of power available to major players.

SEARCHING FOR AN ALTERNATIVE THEORY

Rather than seeing bankruptcy as a technical state in which a firm's debts outweigh its assets, we need to recognize that bankruptcy can be a strategy. This can best be done by an interorganizational perspective that stresses the construction of business crises by large institutions and appreciates the levers of power available to creditors, suppliers, customers, and employees. There are a number of important perspectives that we can draw on to develop an approach to studying bankruptcy as a strategy.

The sociology of business suggests alternative ways of analyzing and interpreting organizational decision-making during a crisis. I think these perspectives can help frame an analysis of organizational behavior during bankruptcy. The managerialist view is quite similar to that of analysts who have always viewed bankruptcy as a choice made solely by management. The resource-dependence and finance-hegemony perspectives, however, suggest alternative ways of looking at corporate decision-making that recognize the power and influence of other institutions in shaping managerial choice. Thus, the latter two paradigms offer new opportunities for developing an intercorporate view of "strategic bankruptcies."

Managerialism

The publication of *The Modern Corporation and Private Property* by Adolf A. Berle, Jr., and Gardiner C. Means in 1932 signaled the beginning of the managerial school. Their main thesis was that the two attributes of ownership—risking wealth to make a profit and the actual managing of the day-to-day activities of the firm—had become divorced. The managerialists took this to mean that control over the corporation had changed hands from the capitalist, driven by the profit motive, to a new class of "professional managers" that could look beyond the bottom line to a host of social concerns.

This supposed "managerial revolution," as James Burnham (1941) called it, occurred as three trends took hold in the U.S. economy: the increasing concentration of corporate power and influence; the increasing dispersion of stock ownership, resulting in a diffusion of control by the owners of capital; and the increasing separation of ownership and control in everyday management of the firm (Berle and Means 1968, xxix).

Managerial theorists over the next three decades developed a theory of organizational behavior based on these developments. With reduced pressure for profits, professional managers were portrayed as having complete control over the corporate enterprise and could look after the interests of their employees as well as the larger commonweal (Berle 1954; Gordon 1945; Kaysen 1957; Marris 1964; Rockefeller 1964). Eventually, managerialists pushed their theory to the logical limit, concluding that, "within a wide range, managerial power is absolute" and "the directoral opinion of corporate managers . . . now chiefly determines the application of risk capital" (Berle 1954, 64, 40).

The managerial school, however, had several major shortcomings. A host of analysts questioned whether the separation of ownership and control was as complete as the managerialists argued (Baran and Sweezy 1966; Baum and Stiles 1965; Kammerschen 1968; Zeitlin 1974; Useem 1980; Glasberg and Schwartz 1983). Moreover, the managerialists' definition of control had always been elusive and ambiguous. Control over the corporation was defined in a variety of ways, including control over wealth, the "actual power to elect the board of directors" of the firm, and the ability to "dictat[e] to management" (Berle and Means 1968, 4, 66), as well as the ability to choose among a wide range of options (Burnham 1941). But rather than actually providing definitive proof of who controlled the corporation, these analysts were really pointing to the exercise of power, and power obviously shifts and is dependent on the particular circumstances of the firm.

The managerialists' assumption that management had nearly absolute independence led to the key weakness of managerial theory: the absence of a theory of *intercorporate* power. Little attention was paid to how other organizations might limit the options that managers choose from.[3]

3. This tendency is analogous to the pluralists' tendency in political theory of focusing on actual decision-making outcomes while ignoring the alternatives that never make it to the public arena (see Alford and Friedland 1985; Eckstein 1990; Lukes 1974).

The managerial perspective permeates some of the literature on business failure and business bankruptcy, inasmuch as many bankruptcy theories similarly fail to employ an intercorporate perspective. Assuming that managers have full control over major corporations, bankruptcy is viewed as a failing of management. Dun & Bradstreet's analysis of the causes of business failure discussed previously is a perfect example of this tendency.

The challenges made to the managerial model in general can also be applied to the managerialist underpinnings of bankruptcy models. The focus on managerial control at the expense of all other organizational actors leads to a truncated view of bankruptcy by concluding that managers both "cause" bankruptcy and "choose" Chapter 11 bankruptcy. (Ironically, in bankruptcy analysis, "choice" usually refers to the final order to file bankruptcy. This definition of choice obviously misses earlier choices that affect the bankruptcy decision and is generally described only as a choice between declaring bankruptcy or voluntarily going out of business.) The emphasis on managerial control underplays the role of other large organizations in shaping the choices available to management at any given time.

Resource Dependency

In sharp contrast to the managerialists, the resource-dependency school began with the central premise that corporations exist in a larger environment composed of other organizations. The classic exposition of this approach suggested that to understand organizational behavior, you must look to "how organizational environments affect and constrain organizations and how organizations respond to external constraints" (Pfeffer and Salancik 1978, xi). Managers are not fully autonomous because they must cope with their environment.[4]

4. The environment is composed of a collection of other organizations run by similarly situated managers.

From this perspective, corporate behavior was seen as managers trying to cope with their environment in order to achieve success (Aldrich 1979; Thompson 1967). The setting of goals was viewed as adapting to the environment (Thompson and McEwen 1958), growth of the organization was a result of properly managing the environment (Starbuck 1965), interlocking directorates were efforts at coopting important segments of the environment (Pfeffer 1972a; Selznick 1966), coalitions and joint ventures were formed to reduce unpredictability in the environment (Thompson and McEwen 1958), and mergers were used by managers to reduce interdependencies with significant members of the environment (Pfeffer 1972b).

Resource dependence quite rightly forced us to look beyond the individual firm to explore the impact of outside forces on organizational behavior. However, the view of the corporation's interaction with the environment tended to be a passive one. That is to say, this view tended to see organizations as adapting to their environment rather than actively manipulating it. From this perspective, bankruptcy could be viewed as a failure of managers to adapt successfully to the environment. While this is almost certainly true to some extent in all bankruptcies, it does not help explain why some firms or industries might be able to alter the conditions of their environments with the support of their creditors (e.g., Braniff Airways as discussed in Mintz and Schwartz 1985, 33–34), while other firms are not afforded this opportunity and are pushed toward bankruptcy (e.g., Manville). A resource-dependence perspective would also have trouble explaining why a firm enters bankruptcy at the moment it does rather than much later or much earlier during the crisis (e.g., W. T. Grant in Glasberg 1982). Most fundamentally, this view would most likely portray bankruptcy as a reaction by management to the environment and underplay the use of bankruptcy as a proactive organizational strategy.

Finance Hegemony

The finance-hegemony school also stressed looking beyond the boundaries of the corporation to understand organizational behavior, but unlike resource-dependence theorists, the finance-hegemony thesis posited the hierarchical dominance of financial institutions (both banks and insurers) over non-financial corporations. Unlike bank-control theory, which argued that banks actually controlled the activities of even the largest corporations (Fitch and Oppenheimer 1970), the finance-hegemony school saw this domination as neither absolute nor deterministic, but rather as episodic.

The power of banks over non-financials results from three peculiarities of capitalist economies: First, finance capital is the universal commodity required by nearly all firms, placing banks in a particularly powerful position. Second, the number of institutions in control of large amounts of this unique commodity is very small. A handful of major banks are therefore in a more unified position than the mass of borrowers. Third, finance capital is unique in that all other commodities are exchanged for a different commodity (today, usually money), whereas finance capital is exchanged only for itself (money is exchanged for more money, to be paid at a later date). Thus, during the period between lending and repayment, the lender has a very keen interest in the activity of the borrower (Mintz and Schwartz 1985).

Some recent work details a variety of mechanisms by which banks exercise power over corporate decision-making. Research has been done on the impact of lending decisions on corporate behavior (Leinsdorf and Etra 1973; Ratcliffe 1979–80; Ratcliffe, Oehler, and Gallops 1979; Ratcliffe, Gallagher, and Ratcliffe 1979). We know that bankers tend to sit on the boards of directors of other corporations more frequently than anyone else (Mintz and Schwartz 1981 and 1985). Research has uncovered some of the mechanisms by which banks exercise power over firms in financial trouble. For example, Davita Glasberg's study of Leasco Corporation

(1981) demonstrates that stock dumping by banks can create corporate crises.

Most important, studies from the resource-dependence and finance-hegemony perspectives have demonstrated that accounting for intercorporate action provides a much richer understanding of institutional action and business crisis. These studies suggest that to understand actions taken in bankruptcy, we must be sure to understand actions taken before the actual bankruptcy filing, since powerful organizations like banks may create the crisis leading to bankruptcy. For example, Glasberg (1982) has shown that in the W. T. Grant bankruptcy, lenders took actions prior to the bankruptcy filing to improve the standing of their loans at the expense of other creditors when bankruptcy was eventually declared. Many of these studies demonstrate the value of an interorganizational approach.

POWER, CONTROL, AND CONSTRAINT DURING BANKRUPTCY

Recognizing the sources of power available to organizations in strategic bankruptcy is essential to fully understanding these cases. Steven Lukes (1974) argues that there are three dimensions of power (see also Bacharach and Baratz 1962). The first dimension is what people usually think of when they hear the word *power:* observable, winner-loser conflicts. In this first dimension, specific outcomes can be studied to determine what individual or group prevailed in a given conflict, usually one occurring in the public arena. Bankruptcy provides a series of such conflicts.

Edward Royce (1985 and 1989) points out that decisions can be made based on the actions of a variety of institutions. The resulting decision can be one that a particular party would have chosen if omnipotent, or it could be one that *none* of the institutions really wanted or is fully satisfied with. Accepting this, the language of causality becomes a bit problematic, in the sense that it is difficult to answer questions like "Who chose the bankruptcy?" (no one person or organization may have chosen it, but it resulted from the various actions of an array of actors); "What was the cause of the bankruptcy filing?" (the actual cause may be the combined actions of members of the firm's immediate environment). But this view *does not* mean that there are no winners and losers in a given bankruptcy case. Simply because no actor or institution gets exactly what it wants does not imply that there are no *relative* winners and losers. Similarly, this view does not mean that all institutions can push equally hard in trying to get their way. Some institutions may have more power than others to push the action in their favor.

The second dimension of power encompasses a whole realm of "non-decisions"—that is, issues that are organized out of the public arena. Institutionalized procedures (the "rules of the game"), along with the predominating values, beliefs, and rituals of society, operate consistently to allow certain issues into the public arena, while others are consistently kept out. What Peter Bacharach and Morton Baratz originally called "non-decision-making," then, is "a means by which demands for change in the existing allocation of benefits and privileges in the community can be suffocated before they are even voiced; or kept covert; or killed before they gain access to the relevant decision-making arena" (Bacharach and Baratz 1970, 44).

According to Lukes, power is also exercised along a third dimension—ideological power. This type of power can prevent people from even considering an idea as possible or practical. Lukes's third dimension might also apply to the bankruptcy process. In the Manville bankruptcy, for example, little consideration was given to the idea of running Manville solely for the benefit of asbestos victims. Apparently, this idea was so foreign to all involved, it would immediately have been ruled out as ludicrous: Who would run such a company? Who would invest in it? This ideological dimension of power thus keeps certain solutions from even being considered in the bankruptcy forum.

Power thus consists of more than observable winner/loser conflicts. It includes things like "authority" (B complies because B recognizes A's command as reasonable); "influence" (A without resorting to threats causes B to change its actions); "effective access" (A is in position to alter B's decision-making apparatus); coercion (A secures B's compliance by the threat of deprivation); and force (A strips B of any choice other than compliance) (for more details see Bacharach and Baratz 1962; Lukes 1974, 1–20). Beth Mintz and Michael Schwartz (1985) add to these the concept of "constraint," in which A, by its actions, alters the profile of options available to B. They provide as an example the decision of the "Big Three" auto manufacturers to enter the spare-parts business when they found they had a large pool of available cash. This action seriously altered the options available to the spare-parts makers who were in a structurally subordinate position to the auto manufacturers. This action constrained the executives of the spare-parts makers and altered their actions.

Obviously, many of these facets of power can be used in combination in the bankruptcy context. Large organizations consistently engage in constraining, coercive, and influencing behavior toward other organizations.

In the case studies to follow, the actions of various institutions in the corporation's network will be assessed using this broad notion of power. My goal is to analyze and assess the various constraining acts of each institution before and during Chapter 11, as well as to determine which institutions or actors seem to win more and which institutions or actors seem to win less.

THE EMBEDDEDNESS OF ORGANIZATIONAL
ACTION DURING BANKRUPTCY

Albert Hirschman points out that economic theory tends to overemphasize perfect and undeviating rational behavior on the part of organizations: "In economics one assumes either fully and undeviatingly rational behavior, or at the very least, an *unchanging level* of rationality." This assumption gets translated into the bankruptcy context as follows: "Economists have typically assumed that a firm that falls behind (or gets ahead) does so for a 'good reason'" (Hirschman 1970, 1, 2). The law-and-economics tradition in legal analysis adopts this assumption of full rationality on the part of organizational actors as they confront bankruptcy law (Baird 1987a and 1987b; Jackson 1986). These theorists would argue that any two firms facing the same economic conditions (i.e., the same levels of assets and debts, the same cash flow, etc.) would react to bankruptcy laws similarly.

However, Mark Granovetter (1985) has pointed out that in understanding and interpreting economic rationality, we must understand the concrete relations among institutional actors in a corporate network. Granovetter's thesis challenges the assumptions of neoclassical economic models and their tendency to assume that rational actors will behave similarly when confronted with similar choices.

Economic decisions are embedded in social structure in at least two ways (see Palmer et al. 1987). First, social relations may cause actors to pursue interests other than those related to the efficiency of a particular course of action. Since competition is seldom perfect (particularly in oligopolistic markets dominated by a few large corporations), efficient options are not always demanded by the market. In addition, knowledge of which course of action is actually *the* most efficient is usually severely bounded. Second, social relations themselves may influence the relative efficiency of the various courses of action. As actors weigh up the relative efficiency of options, presumably they factor in social relations: Will I need this creditor in the future for a loan? How much power do my creditors have? Does my major lender have more power over me than a labor union or a group of asbestos victims? How well can I shape public perceptions of my Chapter 11 filing? Debtors remain eager to please their largest creditors, particularly those creditors with which they might expect to do business again. As a former federal judge, Harold J. Tyler, Jr., has observed, "Debtors in possession are inclined to think of satisfying their big creditors" (*U.S. Code Cong. & Ad. News* 1978a, 5796). "[There is] a natural tendency of a debtor in distress to pacify large creditors, with whom the debtor would expect to do business at the expense of small and scattered public investors" (*U.S. Code Cong. & Ad. News* 1978a, 5796). In this way, large "repeat players" like commercial creditors have an advantage over groups that are less powerful and less organized, like future asbestos victims (Galanter 1974).

Recognizing the embeddedness of social action opens the door to considering issues of power in the shaping of economic rationality in bankruptcy. In strategic bankruptcies, for example, the ability of various institutional actors to shape the relative "efficiency" of the firm's options are crucial determinants of the firm's subsequent actions. Much of the literature on bankruptcy underplays the importance of network relationships in predicting and understanding organizational behavior.

To further complicate matters, the actions of these organizations are themselves embedded in a larger social structure. The salient features of this social structure that shape the very definition of "rational behavior" include the reduction in stigma attached to the bankrupt firm (which reduces the "costs" of bankruptcy) and the changes in federal bankruptcy laws that allow firms to enter bankruptcy earlier, making Chapter 11 a more attractive option to a firm in crisis.

Law plays a large role in shaping what is considered "rational economic behavior" by firms. Changes made to the bankruptcy code in a sweeping legal reform in 1978 altered what we might consider "economically rational behavior" by a firm. Actions considered rational after 1978 (e.g., a Chapter 11 filing) might not have even been contemplated before the changes to the bankruptcy code. Since bankruptcy is a specific, legally institutionalized form of the larger economic phenomenon of "business crisis," we can consider the impact of changes in law and the role of the state in shaping organizational behavior during crisis.

When we are talking about novel business strategies based on new legal rules, a learning process often occurs. All actors, including not just the bankrupt corporation, but also commercial lenders and insurers, suppliers and customers, and the lawyers representing these interests, are testing the new process. It seems foolhardy to expect perfectly rational behavior in such a situation of extreme uncertainty. Rather, actors are *trying* to act rationally as they attempt to define the limits of their actions within a new legal framework. Throughout bankruptcy, institutions are attempting to make what they consider rational decisions. But this rationality is severely bounded. During periods of business crisis, information upon which to base crucial decisions is often just not available. Relaxing the assumption of perfect rationality can bring us to a richer understanding of major bankruptcy cases than is provided by current bankruptcy analyses.

CONCLUSION

The dominant portrayals of the bankruptcy process accept the idea of bankruptcy as last resort and thereby miss the strategic implications of many Chapter 11 filings. The weaknesses inherent in these theories point directly to the importance of moving away from the economic functionalism that has thus far dominated this field of study. By considering the possibility that bankruptcy is used by organizations as a strategy and employing an institutional analysis centering on organizational power, I hope to provide a challenge to conventional views of the role of bankruptcy in society.

In the cases of the Manville Corporation, Continental Airlines, and Texaco, I shall demonstrate that a series of crucial choices were made before and during bankruptcy. These choices shaped the business crisis preceding bankruptcy, helped determine the balance-sheet data of the firm, and "constructed" or "manufactured" the claim to bankruptcy. Thus, the bankruptcy filings resulted from strategic decision-making rather than being passive responses to market forces.

However, these strategic choices can only be understood after accounting for a wide array of organizational actors. These cases involved conflicts between powerful organizations or coalitions of interests: corporations, financial institutions, insurance companies, auditors, health victims, and organized labor. They provide an opportunity to assess the levers of power available to these competing groups as they pursued their interests during bankruptcy. In each of the cases, I try to illuminate the power of institutions to constrain and influence other institutions and individuals.

Despite the broadening of bankruptcy law and the reduction in social stigma attached to the bankrupt, many observers still find it unfathomable that a firm or its creditors would *choose* bankruptcy. In each of the three cases that follow, I shall provide evidence that managers and creditors did indeed mobilize the bankruptcy process in order to transform troublesome ties with other institutions or groups of individuals. These cases thus involve much more than straight economics; they verge on the political: getting rid of a union, resolving a firm's asbestos crisis and avoiding punitive damage awards by channeling asbestos claims into a compensation board system, or reducing court-awarded damages by invoking the bankruptcy process. So although most theorists view bankruptcy as simply a fair, neutral debt-collection process, I think that Chapter 11 is actually an arena where powerful institutions attempt to achieve strategic ends unattainable outside of bankruptcy.

3

The Manville Corporation: Solving Asbestos Liability through Bankruptcy

If you feel sick you go to the doctor; if you're in trouble
you go to the lawyer; and if there is anything else
wrong, you go to the banker.

> —George Scott, First National City
> Bank of New York

It is no surprise that the [Manville Chapter 11] filing
was challenged as a fraud undertaken by Manville
solely to avoid paying the just claims of asbestos
victims.

> —Senator Robert Dole, during Senate
> hearings on the Manville bankruptcy

The Manville Corporation (formerly Johns-Manville) was founded in the 1860s by H. W. Johns. Johns made his fortune from asbestos, a mineral that combines the properties of strength, flexibility, and fire resistance, making it uniquely suited for insulating purposes. In 1925 the company was purchased by Charles Manville, who oversaw rapid expansion as the demand for asbestos rose in such industries as housing and shipbuilding (asbestos proved to be the best material for home insulation and fireproofing in the hulls of large naval vessels).

During this period, the entire asbestos industry began an expansion that was to last through the early 1970s. New uses were discovered for asbestos, including fire-resistant draperies, automobile brake linings, and spray-on insulation. During these years, Manville, the leading asbestos manufacturer, increased its annual sales from $40 million to over $1 billion (Vermeulen and Berman 1982).

Problems with asbestos began to emerge as early as 1906, when a British physician reported the first death caused by exposure to asbestos. Asbestos is a fibrous material. When viewed under a microscope, chrysolite fibers (the most common form of asbestos used commercially) resemble strands of silk (Nelson 1972). If a single fiber is inhaled, it can become embedded in the lung. Over time, the fiber becomes coated with phagocytes, the lung's protective cells, and a fatal tumor may appear (the latency period can be as long as several decades).

Numerous courts, as well as Senate and House subcommittees, have heard arguments over how early the asbestos industry knew of this danger (see U.S. Senate 1982 and especially Brodeur 1985a–e). Critics of the Manville Corporation and lawyers for asbestos victims have argued that Manville knew, or should have known, about the danger of asbestos exposure many decades ago. The asbestos manufacturers, however, claim that they did not know of the danger until 1964, when a landmark study appeared demonstrating that exposure to even the smallest amounts of asbestos may lead to several types of lung cancer (Selikoff 1982).

Armed with new medical evidence and innovative tort liability theories developed through the late 1960s (Berman 1984; Croyle 1978), plaintiffs began filing lawsuits against Manville and other asbestos companies. The pace of litigation against Manville had increased by 1982 to an average filing rate of 3 cases per hour, every hour of every business day. In that year, over 16,500 lawsuits were pending against the Manville Corporation.

Despite this avalanche of lawsuits, Manville remained a highly profitable company. At the end of 1981, the company reported nearly $2 billion in total revenues,[1] ranked high in

---

1. See Manville's financial statement and annual report, December 31, 1981.

the Fortune 500 list, was one of the 30 companies included in the Dow Jones Industrial Average, had a very respectable A3 long-term debt rating from Moody's Investor Services (*Moody's Industrial Manual*, 1982), and held over $600 million in insurance coverage. Manville actively fought those asbestos lawsuits that had made it to court up to that point, and the suits were not yet threatening the financial viability of the company.

Despite the apparent vigor of the corporation, Manville filed for bankruptcy protection under Chapter 11 of the U.S. Bankruptcy Code on August 26, 1982. The Chapter 11 filing caused an outcry from asbestos victims, who felt Manville was trying to escape its liability to its employees, their families, and the firm's customers who had been exposed to the company's harmful products (Asbestos Litigation Group 1983; Vermeulen and Berman 1982). Many observers questioned the motives of a company that portrayed itself as a financially strapped, bankrupt company in its Chapter 11 filing, yet in a full-page advertisement the next day declared to the world, "Nothing is wrong with our businesses."[2] The company's defenders, however, argued that Manville's balance sheet, which included a liability of approximately $2 billion for future asbestos lawsuits, left it with no choice other than bankruptcy. Management was simply responding to the inevitable. Both sides underplayed the importance of the actions taken by other powerful actors in Manville's network.

EVENTS LEADING TO THE BANKRUPTCY FILING

The Insurers Pull Out

According to a variety of sources, Manville had at least $600 million in insurance coverage in the years prior to bankruptcy (see *In re* Asbestos Insurance Coverage Cases Nos. 1072

2. This advertisement appeared in several major U.S. newspapers on August 27, 1982, among them the *New York Times* and the *Washington Post*.

and 765226 [Superior Court for the State of California, March 31, 1980]; *In re* Johns-Manville Corp. 68 B.R. 618 [Bankr. S.D.N.Y. 1986]). The amount of damages paid out before the August 1982 filing did not come close to this figure. Manville should have had no problem continuing business, contesting lawsuits, and paying out on damage awards using its extensive insurance coverage.

But beginning in the late 1970s, Manville's insurance carriers, led by the Travelers Corporation, began refusing to pay out on awards. The central issue in this legal dispute was the "trigger date" of insurance coverage. Between World War I and the early 1980s, Manville carried numerous insurance policies with more than twenty different insurance companies. Legal doctrine remained unclear as to which insurance firm should cover a particular award in a given case: the insurer during the *exposure* of the victim, the insurer during the *manifestation* of the disease, the insurer during the *filing* of the lawsuit, the insurer during the *judgment* of the case, or some combination of these. Since the symptoms of asbestosis often do not appear until decades after exposure, more than one insurance company was potentially liable in most of the 16,500 cases.

For their part, the insurance companies sounded like a Tower of Babel, agreeing on only one thing: the correct theory of coverage was *not* the one that made them pay the damage award in a given case (*In re* Asbestos Insurance Coverage Cases [1980]). While there was a clear illogic to their collective voice (i.e., although Manville had had continuous insurance coverage, no one was responsible for any given claim), the process of untangling each case involved massive legal resources and huge delays in payments, since the insurers controlled a key asset, capital, in the form of insurance reserves, at least until forced to pay by the courts. So because legal doctrine was unclear at the time and because the insurance companies were in a powerful position vis-à-vis Manville, the insurers were able to escape paying on claims at least temporarily. When the insurers refused to pay, necessitating vast expenditures to shake loose insurance payments through the legal system, they severely limited Manville's options. This was the beginning of the crisis, Manville's vice president and corporate counsel told a Senate subcommittee: "The failure of our insurance carriers to provide interim funding—even on a basis fully reserving their right in the event of a judicial determination favorable to their position—was a major contributing factor which compelled Manville to file Chapter 11" (U.S. Senate 1982, 30–31).

If the insurers had been less powerful or not acted as a group, Manville might have been able to force their hand more quickly and gotten them to provide insurance coverage.

The State Refuses to Intervene

Manville found itself in a difficult position. Plaintiffs began to win ever larger judgments against the firm, and it was unable to tap its sizable insurance coverage. The firm found itself facing a growing cash-flow crisis (Brodeur 1985a–e).

As the asbestos crisis grew through the 1970s, Manville consistently argued that the government should provide a legislative solution to the asbestos problem in the form of a superfund to compensate victims of exposure. Manville's position was that "the majority of overexposure to asbestos took place in government-owned or controlled shipyards, where asbestos insulations were installed [in naval ships]" (*Manville Facts* [internal document, May 1984]). G. Earl Parker, Manville V.P., argued that "the federal government's behavior in all critical respects shows it to be as liable a tortfeasor as any other entity" (U.S. House of Representatives 1982).

Manville buttressed its claim with the fact that the United States was a defendant or third-party defendant in over 1,200 asbestos liability actions, involving nearly 13,000 individual claims. Approximately 80 percent of these third-party lawsuits involved government-owned or private ship-yards (U.S. House of Representatives 1982; U.S. Senate 1982).

The bill that Manville supported (the Asbestos Workers Recovery Act) would have been useful to Manville in two ways. First, it mandated compensation for all victims from a fund equally financed by the federal government and the asbestos manufacturers. Since the government would con-tribute a large sum of money, the fund promised to reduce the overall amount that Manville would have to pay to vic-tims. Ultimately, Manville would be likely to pay less money through a compensation board system than through the court system (Croyle 1978; Johnson and Heler 1984).

Second, and more important, the bill would have placed a cap on total liability; that is, a large fund would be set up, and victims would draw only from this pool (similar to the Agent Orange fund). The fund would give Manville a better idea of its total future liability, facilitating corporate plan-ning and access to credit, since Manville's lenders and insur-ers would also have liked to know that the liability had a quantifiable limit.

As the crisis worsened through the late 1970s and early 1980s, Manville increased its efforts to gain congressional approval of the Asbestos Workers Recovery Act (AWRA), but was unable to achieve passage of the bill. It is interesting to compare this episode with Chrysler's successful attempt at obtaining a federal bailout (Glasberg 1983; Turkel 1982). One of the most conspicuous differences between the two cases is that the commercial lenders were not as active in pushing the Manville bill as they appear to have been in the Chrysler case. This could be explained by the fact that the lenders in the Manville case saw Chapter 11 as a possible option, given the legal changes made in 1978. Commercial lenders stood to lose hundreds of millions of dollars if asbestos victims began to win their cases in various courts around the coun-try and Manville was drained of its remaining assets. Apparently, they decided that Chapter 11 reorganization was preferable to allowing Manville to continue business as usual while fighting the lawsuits.

Manville made the strategic mistake of trying to implicate the tobacco companies as partners in the fund, since smoking greatly increases the chance of getting asbestosis. This alienated powerful congressional members from tobacco states, who refused to support the bill.

Despite a series of hearings in both the House and the Senate, Manville could not gain passage of AWRA. In fact, the government continued to contest its own tort liability in the asbestos crisis: "It is the position of the government that it bears no other financial responsibility [other than the Federal Employees Compensation Act and the Longshoreman's and Harbor Workers' Compensation Act] to these workers."[3]

The Auditors and the "Rules of Accounting"

With no readily available insurance and no chance of a government superfund, Manville found itself in a difficult position. However, Manville's president and chief operating officer, Frederick Pundsack, continued to oppose declaring bankruptcy vigorously, contending that Manville was still "a viable, ongoing business enterprise" (Chen 1984, 30). The financial community, however, saw things differently, and this proved to be a decisive factor in the decision to declare bankruptcy.

Manville's accountants, Coopers & Lybrand, qualified the firm's annual report. This qualification was essentially a footnote that acknowledged the potential liability from asbestos-related lawsuits but stated that the damages could not be accurately estimated at the time of the filing (Manville Corporation, annual report, 1981). This qualification thus exempted Manville from the Financial Accounting Stan-

3. Quoted from a letter received by the author from B. Wayne Vance, assistant attorney general for the United States, Civil Division, dated September 25, 1984.

dards Board Opinion Number 5, "Accounting for Contingencies."[4] FASB Rule Number 5 requires "the booking of a reserve when a contingent liability becomes probable and its amount can be estimated" (U.S. House of Representatives 1982). Since future liabilities were deemed inestimable, Manville was not required by the SEC to put aside collateral equal to the liability.

Ironically, this footnote, which exempted Manville from setting aside money for future claims, had some adverse consequences for the company. Such a qualification is not removed from an audit report until the potential debit (in this case the potential liability) has been properly estimated and an adequate reserve has been established. In Manville's case, the reserve would have had to be enormous once the liability was estimated. Such a reserve would place massive constraints on the firm's ability to function, because it could only be funded by liquidating a substantial portion of the company's assets. Thus, once the qualification was attached to the annual report, Manville could not remove it without either achieving a favorable settlement with insurers or selling off assets to accumulate a large reservoir of "liquid capital."

The Power of Creditors

The action of the auditors had no immediate impact, but it indicated that the financial community had lost confidence in Manville's strategy of aggressively fighting asbestos cases in court, continuing business as usual, and paying its creditors on time. Soon afterward, Manville's long-term debt rating was lowered from B to Ca by Moody's Investor Service (*Moody's Industrial Manual*, 1982; 1983). This was a serious blow, because a Ca rating, considered below investment

4. The Financial Accounting Standards Board (FASB) promulgates reporting and disclosure principles used by the accounting profession and supported by the Securities and Exchange Commission (see Copeland et al. 1980).

grade, usually leads creditors to refuse to loan money to a firm at competitive rates. The lowered rating thus promised to increase Manville's interest payments dramatically.

Ironically, nothing had changed substantially in Manville's financial condition except that the auditors had placed the qualification on the report and creditors now had justification for refusing to loan money to the firm. At a Senate hearing, G. Earl Parker, Manville's vice president, highlighted the devastating effect the qualification and the lenders' collective decision had on the firm:

> Our auditors would not remove this qualification of our annual report until we forecast our asbestos-health liabilities. The effects of a qualified report on a public company are significant and adverse. Many investors will not purchase any securities from, or make any loans to, any company whose report is qualified. Other investors will do so only at premium rates. Our investment banking advisors told us that, until our asbestos-health claims were resolved, there was simply no way for Manville to raise any significant amount of expansion capital anywhere in world markets. (U.S. Senate 1982, 22–23)

The possibility loomed that Manville's creditors would begin accelerating payments on Manville's $315 million in long-term debt. Without access to credit markets, such acceleration would have driven Manville into involuntary bankruptcy.[5] Even without accelerated loan payments, Manville would have trouble operating without access to credit at competitive rates. The firm had been moving into new areas, such as forest products, since losing its once-lucrative asbestos revenues. It could not continue this essential di-

---

5. Involuntary bankruptcy usually requires the appointment of a trustee to oversee the company during reorganization and is much less favorable to the debtor than a voluntary Chapter 11 filing. One bankruptcy attorney I interviewed told me that large lenders prefer to pressure a firm into voluntary bankruptcy (by calling in loans or accelerating payments) rather than forcing involuntary bankruptcy. Triggering involuntary bankruptcy makes the lender vulnerable to lawsuits challenging the action. This problem would not be encountered if the firm itself filed the bankruptcy petition.

versification once the qualification was placed in the 1981 report.

The Board of Directors

In early August 1982, Manville's newly appointed CEO, John McKinney, formed a subcommittee of the board of directors composed of John Schroeder, a retired vice-chairman of Morgan Guaranty Trust (Manville's commercial banker for over fifty years); William May, dean of New York University's graduate business school; and Charles Zwick, CEO of Southeast Banking Corporation (Brodeur 1985d, 47). This committee quickly replaced Coopers & Lybrand with Price Waterhouse as Manville's auditor. Within weeks, Price Waterhouse approved a Manville filing to the Securities and Exchange Commission that stated that the future liabilities owing to asbestos could now be accurately estimated and reserved for according to FASB Rule Number 5. Manville commissioned an epidemiological estimate of the incidence and severity of asbestos-related diseases attributable to its products. A consulting firm estimated that the total number of claims would be 52,000, at a cost to Manville of approximately $2 billion, about the amount of Manville's total assets (Epidemiological Resources Inc. 1982; *Manville Facts* [internal document, May 1984]). The estimate and SEC filing cleared the way for Manville's voluntary Chapter 11 filing, since the company now claimed that it was in a state of "equity insolvency"; that is, it would not be able to meet future liabilities as they came due. In Manville's 10Q filing with the SEC, the firm noted:

> Absent filing for protection under Chapter 11, the company would have been required to record a liability for the projected cost of the A-H [asbestos-health] claims and future A-H claims in accordance with the Statement of Financial Accounting Standards No. 5, "Accounting for Contingencies." Such a liability would have substantially eliminated the company's net worth and would have enabled lenders to accelerate substantially all of the Company's medium and long-term

debt. (Securities and Exchange Commission, Manville Corporation Form 10Q, § II-4, March 31, 1985)

Manville had previously agreed to loan covenants that called for the acceleration of loan payments if the firm tried to book a reserve large enough to cover the projected asbestos costs (*Manville Facts*, May 1984).

MANVILLE FILES FOR BANKRUPTCY

Manville filed for bankruptcy on August 26, 1982. The filing raised eyebrows across the country, inasmuch as Manville still held assets in excess of $2 billion. Many commentators asked, "How is it possible for an apparently sound company to declare bankruptcy?" (Asbestos Litigation Group 1983; Vermeulen and Berman 1982).

I think that Manville's filing actually did fit the letter and the spirit of the Bankruptcy Code of 1978, although carried to its logical extreme (Delaney 1985). As we have already seen, one of the major arguments leveled at the old Bankruptcy Act of 1898 was that by the time a firm was able to seek relief (under old Chapter X), it was often beyond salvation. The main goal of the new code was to allow for successful debtor rehabilitation (Roe 1984, 895). The Senate and House reports on the new code make clear that the intent of Congress was to broaden the conditions under which a firm could file for Chapter 11 protection, thereby improving the chances of the firm reemerging as a viable concern (Delaney 1985).

Manville, in its debtor affidavit to the court, demonstrated that it understood the intentions of the new code and intended to carry them to an extreme that Congress had perhaps not envisioned when it broadened the code: "It is thus Manville's intention to formulate effective procedures to accomplish precisely that in a manner which will not improperly favor any creditor over any other creditor similarly situated, be consistent with the fundamental bankruptcy tenet of equality of distribution and permit Manville to emerge as the viable and profitable business it has been and expects to be once again" (Manville's debtor affidavit accompanying *In re* Johns-Manville Corp. [1986]).

Manville called on a series of financial experts to demonstrate that its liabilities extending into the distant future would overwhelm its assets. Although these estimates are extremely difficult to make and are almost always based on a series of arguable assumptions, Manville was granted Chapter 11 status. All asbestos lawsuits were immediately "stayed" (put on hold) pending a reorganization plan (Delaney 1989b).

THE PROPOSED REORGANIZATION PLAN

By 1987, Manville, which had been under Chapter 11 protection for over five years, had settled upon the basic outline of its financial reorganization. Under the plan, Manville's commercial creditors were granted full payment on the money owed to them and a package of stocks, warrants, and bonds valued at $200 million in lieu of interest. "This is all an effort to make more money available to creditors," a Manville spokesman stated (*NYT*, April 23, 1986, D5). In addition, creditor pressure forced the resignation of Manville's president, J. T. Hulce, and Manville named its chief financial officer, W. Thomas Stephens, as its new president. Given his financial background, Stephens was preferred over Hulce by the financial community (*Business Week*, May 12, 1986, 36; July 7, 1986, 76–77).

In sum, the commercial creditors received all the money owed them, were given stocks in place of interest, and had their choice guiding the firm. These outcomes may help explain the active role of Morgan Guaranty's John Schroeder in pushing for the bankruptcy filing. The commercial creditors were able to get their money back relatively quickly and could now loan money to Manville at higher rates and with restrictive covenants. In other words, they could factor in the future risk of Manville returning to bankruptcy court should the epidemiological estimates prove wrong.

Morgan Guaranty, Manville's lead lender, had in fact been doing just this in the years prior to bankruptcy. In 1979 Morgan had arranged a $100 million offering of notes due in 1985 that contained covenants restricting the incurrence of any secured debt that would have higher priority for repayment in the bankruptcy court (see Johns-Manville Corp. and Morgan Guaranty Trust Co. of New York, Trustee, Indenture dated as of May 1, 1979; Roe 1984, 857). This type of clause limiting a company's ability to create secured debt is the most common covenant found in unsecured debt offerings (see McDaniel 1983, 867–68).

Current and future asbestos victims were granted a pool of capital in excess of $2 billion, funded by contributions from Manville's insurers and from a portion of Manville's profits each year for twenty-seven years. While this figure might seem like a large sum, it allowed for only $30,000 to $50,000 for each of the estimated 40,000 to 60,000 asbestos claims. Nevertheless, the official asbestos claimants' group voted for the plan, apparently reasoning that after a five-year delay in bankruptcy proceedings, this was the best they were likely to do.

Manville's common stockholders lost up to 80 percent of the value of their stock in a "reverse split," in which six shares of stock were traded for a single share, "thereby fattening the pot for creditors and vastly reducing shareholder equity in the company" (*NYT*, April 23, 1986, D5). Shareholders receive a lower priority in bankruptcy court than other creditors such as banks and asbestos claimants. This means that shareholders are only paid after more senior priority layers are compensated in full. It was therefore somewhat surprising that Manville's shareholders received even 20 percent of the value of their holdings. Given the epidemiological estimates of asbestosis and cancer claims, however, the court ruled that shareholders could retain 20 percent of their claims. If the estimates turn out to be wrong, and the compensation fund runs out of money, the shareholders will have had an opportunity to sell their stock and get their money out. The financial risk has thus been placed on the shoulders of the future victims, who must count on both the accuracy of the estimates of asbestosis *and* the profitability of Manville for three decades. Unlike commercial lenders, asbestos victims were not able to gain restrictive covenants on corporate behavior to enhance their chances of recovery in bankruptcy court.

Future financial risk was also shifted to other, smaller asbestos manufacturers who did not enter bankruptcy. During Manville's five years under Chapter 11 court protection, individuals were blocked from suing Manville. Many of these asbestos victims sued other asbestos companies, since victims were often exposed to asbestos from several manufacturers. Companies outside the Chapter 11 process therefore had to continue contesting and paying out on asbestos suits.

Shareholders strongly protested against the plan in bankruptcy court and were the only group to vote against it. Although in theory all parties must approve a reorganization plan, there is an aptly named procedure in the bankruptcy code called "cram down" that may be invoked:

> If any impaired class of creditors or equity holders does not accept a plan but all of the other requirements of the Bankruptcy Code are met, the proponent of the plan may invoke the so-called "cram down" provisions of the Bankruptcy Code. Under these provisions, the Bankruptcy Court may confirm a plan notwithstanding the non-acceptance of the plan by an impaired class of creditors or equity security holders if certain requirements of the Bankruptcy Code are met. (Securities and Exchange Commission, Manville Corporation Form 10Q, § II-19, March 31, 1985)

The plan was thus confirmed in spite of the dissent by shareholders. A lawyer representing this group stated, "The company decided to give interest to the commercial creditors and they decided to take it out of the shareholders' hide" (*NYT*, April 23, 1986, D5). This lawyer failed to recognize that

Manville did not make this decision in a vacuum. Its actions resulted from an interplay between its own decisions and numerous other decisions of important and powerful institutions in its immediate network.

CONSTRUCTING THE CLAIM TO BANKRUPTCY

Economic functionalists might be able to take Manville's balance sheet on the day of the Chapter 11 filing and argue that Manville had no other choice than to declare bankruptcy. In fact, any decent bankruptcy-prediction model among those discussed in chapter 2 would find that the level of liabilities and assets on that balance sheet implied bankruptcy. This, however, misses the crucial actions prior to bankruptcy in which various institutional actors helped to shape the calculation of the firm's assets and liabilities. Commercial creditors and the company and its auditors made important choices that ensured the claim to bankrupt status. In the Manville case, the interesting question really was not "Do liabilities outweigh assets? but rather "When does a liability *become* a liability?" That is to say, when do future asbestos liabilities become recognized and acted upon as real liabilities by the firm, its creditors, and the bankruptcy court?

This case illustrates the danger of macroeconomic models' unquestioned acceptance of balance-sheet data. Much of what wound up on Manville's balance sheet (the "official assets and liabilities," if you will) was actually socially constructed by various institutional actors in Manville's network. The power and influence of actors in the corporate network actually shaped the crisis itself, precipitating the bankruptcy filing.

Contrary to the dominant theories of corporate bankruptcy, Manville's decision to file under Chapter 11 was not simply made by management in response to market forces and an unfavorable asset-to-debt ratio that left the firm with no choice but Chapter 11 bankruptcy. Certainly, there was a very real component to Manville's financial problems. The company faced over 16,000 lawsuits when it filed for bankruptcy in August 1982. However, it is also clear that the lawsuits had not yet threatened a substantial portion of the firm's assets, which still exceeded $2 billion at the time of the filing. The company could have continued contesting asbestos lawsuits without declaring bankruptcy. In fact, Manville's departing CEO, Frederick Pundsack, argued right up to the filing against the bankruptcy in a letter to his successor: "[The filing] is wrong for our stockholders, wrong for our employees, wrong for our creditors, wrong for our customers, and wrong for our suppliers" (Brodeur 1985d, 48).

Several elements of the case point to the strategic nature of the bankruptcy filing and to the choices Manville made to ensure approval of its Chapter 11 filing. First, the epidemiological estimates commissioned by Manville rested on a series of arguable assumptions. The authors of the study acknowledged that the actual number of lawsuits the company might face could be "as low as half or as much as twice the number our calculations suggest" (Brodeur 1985d, 42). Manville could have continued to argue that the estimates were not reliable and remained out of bankruptcy court.

Second, and more important, Manville did not commission the epidemiological studies until shortly before its Chapter 11 petition. Manville could have done the estimates several years earlier or delayed the study until several years later.

Third, FASB Rule Number 5 may appear technically written and empirically definable, but it actually allows some latitude for interpreting exactly when a future tort liability becomes calculable. This permits wide discretion on the part of the company and its auditors in deciding how to comply with the rule. Manville's liabilities were not judged as estimable in 1979 or 1980, but were suddenly deemed estimable in 1982, just prior to the Chapter 11 filing.

Up to a certain point in time, Manville's future asbestos liability was not treated as real in terms of SEC and accounting requirements. This case demonstrates that we should distinguish between a liability (there is damage, and the firm will be held responsible monetarily) and an "official liability" (the liability is recognized as official and real by important social institutions—the Securities and Exchange Commission, the Federal Accounting Standards Board, the Internal Revenue Service).

When an existing liability becomes an official liability can only be understood by accounting for the actions of the lenders and insurers. Manville's creditors, insurers, auditors, and the federal government all played crucial roles in Manville's bankruptcy. Why Manville chose to commission the epidemiological studies and to declare bankruptcy when it did can only be understood by looking at the role of these actors.

Prior to the bankruptcy filing, Manville's relationship with its workers and other asbestos victims introduced a major strain into Manville's network as these victims began to sue the company. The asbestos crisis, by introducing a large uncertainty into the network, led to sharp alterations in other network ties. Each of these relationships assumed a pivotal role at different times during the drama.

Mounting lawsuits led Manville to activate its insurance policies, transforming a formerly routine relationship into a contentious one. As soon as the insurers refused to cover damage awards, Manville was forced to use its own reserves to cover court judgments in favor of asbestos victims. The insurers, by refusing to cover claims, pushed Manville toward bankruptcy. Mintz and Schwartz (1985) argue that insurance companies, with their command of large reserves of capital, hold a powerful position in the general economy. However, they have not specified when insurers are able to exercise this dominance, particularly vis-à-vis powerful corporations. This case suggests that on some occasions major corporations may face financial distress requiring a large infusion of insurance payments and that routine processes may not guarantee these payments. This circumstance may activate the latent power of insurers. Manville was unsuccessful in its attempt to wrest the insurance coverage it was legally entitled to owing to its subordinate position vis-à-vis its insurers.

Manville also attempted to transform its relationship with the government, trying to make it a partner in the resolution of the crisis. The federal government's decision not to provide money to asbestos victims closed yet another door to Manville. While Chrysler's bailout has received much notice, the federal government's refusal to provide money to Manville has not been addressed. The Manville case indicates that the state does not always intervene in dramatic fashion to settle disputes between factions of capital, but instead provides a variety of arenas for these potential conflicts. Each arena has its own history and biases. The changes in the 1978 law have allowed organizations to choose bankruptcy court as the forum in which crucial social issues are decided. Once Congress refused a bailout, Manville and its commercial creditors preferred the arena of bankruptcy court (with its stress on the preservation of private capital) to the arena of tort liability (which is more likely to stress protection for individual health victims).

These closed doors introduced uncertainty into Manville's relationship with its accountants and, in turn, with its commercial lenders. The role of the auditor was certainly a curious one. Coopers & Lybrand had qualified Manville's annual reports through 1980, stating that the asbestos liability could not be estimated. These qualifications allowed Manville to keep the future asbestos liability off its balance sheet (since it was not yet estimated) and stay out of bankruptcy. The new auditor, hired by the subcommittee of the board of directors just weeks before the Chapter 11 filing, approved a 1982 SEC filing that argued that the liability was now estimable. This paved the way for Manville's argument that it was in a state of equity insolvency.[6]

6. Recent lawsuits against accounting firms by major banks are an indication of how important auditors are for providing "warning signals" of corporate financial distress to the banking community (*Business Week*, May 13, 1985, 128–30; *Newsday*, April 21, 1985, 100; *Newsweek*, December 3, 1984, 72).

The decision by Manville's commercial creditors to loan the firm money only at extremely high interest rates (if at all) made it difficult for Manville to compete in world markets. The national interest rate mattered little to Manville; what mattered was the particular decision made by creditors to withhold loan capital. Thus, commercial creditors, through their control of capital, play a crucial role in pushing financially troubled firms toward bankruptcy.

The Manville case suggests that directors can become extremely important during times of corporate crisis. Research on corporate interlocks has long suffered from a lack of specific evidence of the importance of interlocking directorates on day-to-day decision-making at the firm.[7] The Manville case provides one very significant piece of evidence in this regard. While there is no evidence that Morgan's Schroeder played an important role in decision-making at Manville before the asbestos crisis, as the crisis worsened, he assumed a pivotal role. Schroeder headed the committee that hired the new auditors, who in turn deemed the asbestos liability as estimable (Brodeur 1985d). During times of potential crisis, it appears that directors from financial institutions can step up to engage in actual decision-making.

Manville's lenders withheld future loan capital and threatened to recall existing loans. These activities could ultimately have led to drastic and fundamental alterations in Manville's relations with its suppliers and customers—that is, an inability to pay suppliers and deliver finished goods to customers.

---

7. A large literature suggests the importance of interlocks (Bearden 1982; Glasberg and Schwartz 1983; Mizruchi 1982). But, as Edward Herman (1973, 1979, and 1981) argues, there is little direct evidence regarding the impact on the firm. Mintz and Schwartz (1985) counter that interlocks are "information conduits," providing financial institutions with information to manage the flow of capital. This case suggests that in addition to providing information on the health of the firm, corporate directors can assume pivotal roles at times when management is weak (e.g., faced with large liabilities). Schroeder, Manville's major interlock with its lead lender, Morgan Guaranty, assumed a key role in heading the group that hired the new auditor (Brodeur 1985e).

Faced with these constraints and the inability to re-transform these "corporate life-threatening" relationships into more stable ones, Manville opted for a Chapter 11 filing in order to resolve its asbestos nightmare. Chapter 11 provided a structured setting in which Manville was successful in achieving changes it was unable to achieve outside of the bankruptcy process. Rather than a mechanism to ensure economic efficiency, bankruptcy in this case provided an opportunity for management to reduce threats to certain ties with powerful institutions drastically. Although fraught with risks, Chapter 11 provided a structured setting for a firm to transform troublesome, "corporate life-threatening" relationships into more stable, controllable ones.

The Chapter 11 filing eliminated the creditors' threats of a loan recall, since all loan payments were "stayed" during the bankruptcy process. Similarly, payments to asbestos victims were also postponed during the five years Manville spent under Chapter 11 protection. This five-year respite from asbestos damage awards and loan payments favored Manville by giving it the time to settle its claims against insurers, providing the company once again with its full insurance coverage.

The reorganization plan removed the uncertainty of the tort liability system where asbestos victims could potentially win ever larger judgments, particularly as more damaging evidence emerged against Manville. More important, the reorganization plan did not allow for any punitive damages against the company. The uncertainty of the tort system was replaced with a compensation board system, favored by Manville, its commercial lenders, and its insurers alike. The certainty of knowing its future liabilities will help routinize Manville's relationship with its commercial creditors and has given the company access to credit once again.

Manville's internal decision-making processes and its relationship to general market forces are thus not as important to understanding its actions as are its relationships with various institutional actors in its immediate network. However, the dominant economic perspective on corporate bankruptcy would argue that *any* firm faced with the same balance-sheet data (the same liabilities and assets) and the same macroeconomic conditions (stage in the business cycle, national interest rates, etc.) might be expected to make the same choice (whether to declare bankruptcy or not)—assuming, of course, that firms act rationally. I would argue that knowing the balance-sheet figures and macroeconomic factors is not nearly enough either to make this prediction successfully in any given case or, more important, to understand organizational behavior during a crisis. What must also be assessed are the nature of network relationships, the specific ties of the firm, and the relative power of each actor in the network. This case illustrates that definitions of such seemingly indisputable terms as *liability*, *debt*, *asset*, and *insolvent* can switch over time according to the power and interests of various institutional actors.

The reorganization plan did not simply allow more efficient collection on valid claims. The plan also shifted financial risk to the most vulnerable (and unorganized) group— future asbestos victims. Since Manville's liability to future victims was so difficult to estimate and extended far into the future, the financial risk of misestimation was shifted from commercial creditors to the future asbestos victims. Asbestos victims will only be able to collect if Manville can continue to fund the compensation fund for the next three decades. If Manville is unable to remain sufficiently profitable, or if the number of victims was underestimated, the future asbestos claimants will be unable to collect. Commercial lenders were able to get their money out of the firm fairly quickly. Should they decide to loan Manville money in the future, they can factor in the risk of Manville returning to bankruptcy court or liquidating by charging Manville higher interest rates, providing only secured lending (with a higher priority in court than asbestos claims) and restrictive loan covenants. Thus, in this case, bankruptcy acted less as a neutral market mechanism or neutral debt-collection system and more as a political arena in which powerful organizations tried to shift financial burden and future financial risk to weaker parties.

In fact, this is exactly what has happened since the firm's emergence from Chapter 11. The compensation board, funded on a yearly basis, announced that it would run out of money for fiscal year 1989 sometime during the second or third quarter of the fiscal year. This meant that health claimants had to wait until the first quarter of the next fiscal year to collect on claims. A waiting period of six months is crucial to someone dying of asbestosis. The compensation board has continued to run into problems because both the number and severity of claims were underestimated in the reorganization plan.

The importance of the 1978 bankruptcy reform became crystal clear in this case. The broad definition of *claim* in the new code allowed for the seemingly curious situation of a firm with a large pool of capital declaring Chapter 11 bankruptcy based on estimated liabilities that loom in the distant future. This case demonstrates that changes in bankruptcy law can lead to changes in organizational behavior and indeed can change what behavior is deemed economically rational. Changes in the legal context of business crises become crucial to the meaning of *bankrupt*.

Legal changes paved the way for a class of cases in which future assets and debts were used as the measuring stick for the determination of bankruptcy. A. H. Robins gained bankruptcy court approval of a fund, similar to Manville's, to compensate women injured by the Dalkon Shield intrauterine device. Like the Manville case, victims claim they will get less from the bankruptcy settlement than through the tort system.

Additional factors that may have affected the bankruptcy decision and that are not normally considered in market models of bankruptcy include the firm's ability to manage its corporate image during bankruptcy and to gain acceptance of its own definition of the situation ("bankrupt but not *really* bankrupt"), the closeness of ties with commercial creditors, and the existence of a vulnerable group (e.g., future asbestos victims, labor) to shift financial risk to.

4

Continental Airlines: Using Bankruptcy to Abrogate Union Contracts

We view Chapter 11 as the end of the line, the last resort.

—*Frank Lorenzo, CEO of Continental Airlines, testifying in bankruptcy court*

We don't trust him. Frankly, we think he's a little short on corporate integrity.

—*Captain Henry A. Duffy, president of the Air Line Pilots Association, referring to Frank Lorenzo*

In 1936 a charismatic high school dropout named Robert Six borrowed $90,000 from a relative and bought a 40 percent interest in Varney Air Transport, a mail courier. Robert Six soon became president of the three-plane company and changed its name to Continental Air Lines.[1] Six was an aviation enthusiast and soon grew tired of flying planes simply to carry mail. He made the decision to begin carrying passengers at a time when commercial passenger aviation was still in its infancy. But the decision was made at precisely the right time. Six bought a small fleet of twin-engine planes and began passenger service in Texas and a few surrounding states.

1. This section draws, in part, on material from Murphy 1986 and Serling 1974.

Within twenty years, Continental had grown to twenty-one planes serving thirty-six cities. Six had a reputation in the industry as a man who kept on the forefront of modern aviation, an executive who always wanted to have the latest aircraft in his Continental fleet. As a result airline pilots throughout the industry held Continental in high regard. A major turning point for Continental came when the company was awarded a license from the Civil Aeronautics Board to the growing Los Angeles–Denver–Chicago route. This route was to provide the cornerstone for Continental's success in the 1960s and 1970s.

These two decades proved to be "go-go" years for the airline industry as a whole. Continental, with a solid share of the LA–Denver–Chicago route, rose right along with the rest of the industry. Continental's revenues climbed steadily and impressively from $46 million in 1958 to $775 million in 1978, and the company occupied ninth or tenth place among U.S. airlines throughout these favorable years (Murphy 1986, 2).

Along with revenue increases, Continental also experienced steady increases in profitability, maintaining one of the highest profit margins in the industry. Robert Six stuck to his belief in keeping revenue and profits high through technological superiority linked with high-quality service. Six was the first to offer jet aircraft on the LA–Denver–Chicago route, and as a result, kept 25 percent of the market against competition from the two powerhouses of the industry: United Airlines and American Airlines (Murphy 1986, 3).

According to popular accounts, Continental and Six managed also to maintain a "remarkable *esprit de corps*" (Murphy 1986, 4). Many Continental employees seemed to feel that they worked for the "class organization" of the industry. This attitude seems to have resulted from several factors. First, the regulated airline industry allowed for fairly high pay, leading to a generally high level of job satisfaction among most in the airline industry at the time. Second, Six was genuinely an inspiring leader, often visiting airplane cockpits to chat with the pilots. Third, Six's philosophy of getting the newest aircraft before the competition dovetailed with the pilots' professional interest in aviation advances. Continental's relationship with its major unions seemed downright cordial as well. A president of the International Association of Machinists' local said of those days, "[Our relationship] was almost like a marriage" (Murphy 1986, 5).

Although many of the popular accounts of Continental have a mythlike quality and are probably overplayed, it does seem apparent that during the boom years for airlines, Continental enjoyed both financial success and good relations with its employees. Of course, this is a much easier achievement in an industry that is booming. Most airlines during these years were enjoying remarkable success, and working in the industry was seen as both a lucrative career and somehow romantic.

However, airline deregulation was just around the corner.

DEREGULATION OF THE AIRLINE INDUSTRY

President Franklin Roosevelt set up the Civil Aeronautics Board in 1938. The CAB would soon make airlines the most regulated industry in the country. For forty years, the CAB, with very few exceptions, refused to approve any applications for new airlines to fly major routes. The "Big Four"— United, American, TWA, and Eastern—held "grandfather" rights to the lucrative transcontinental flights. Anthony Sampson in *Empires of the Sky* (1984) details the cozy relationship between CAB members and airline executives. Political influence apparently played a large role in the awarding of routes during the days of regulation. Robert Six, for example, hired Pierre Salinger to run his international division at a time when Continental was trying desperately to get rights to a route across the Pacific. Salinger, of course, had a close relationship with President Lyndon Johnson, who did indeed agree to award the route to Continental. However, when Richard Nixon succeeded Johnson, he overturned the award, apparently at the urging of Robert Haldeman, who was said to have a grudge against Salinger (see Sampson 1984, 133–35).

The CAB often made decisions that seemed to hurt the individual consumer and help the oligopolistic airlines. Secor Brown, CAB chairman from 1969 to 1973, in fact, spoke in favor of what he called "intelligent oligopoly" (Sampson 1984, 135). The CAB legitimated the oligopoly by arguing that it was ensuring service to smaller cities across the country by forcing airlines to serve those routes. In exchange, the CAB provided regulated, stable, and lucrative pricing.

During the 1970s, pressure for deregulation came from a pair of strange bedfellows: increasingly vocal opponents of "big government" and pro-consumer liberals. Democrats and Republicans raced to claim the mantle of deregulation. Senator Edward Kennedy held Senate hearings to look at the relationship between the airlines and the CAB. Meanwhile, President Gerald Ford tried to grab the issue back by stressing free enterprise and the reduction of "big government."

President Jimmy Carter, however, is the person remembered as the "Great Deregulator." Under his leadership, the deregulation movement culminated in the Airline Deregulation Act of 1978, which changed the airline industry forever. The act introduced competitive pricing and eliminated federal subsidies to airlines. The act detailed a six-year program to remove regulations from the industry. In fact, the program envisioned abolishing the CAB altogether by 1985.

One commentator has called the act "the beginning of the greatest upheaval in American air transport since the thirties" (Sampson 1984, 136). Almost immediately, business and financial entrepreneurs set up small, non-union airlines to exploit limited market niches, such as flying short shuttle flights on frequently traveled routes like New York to Washington or Boston. These small carriers provided "no frills" service at rock-bottom prices. The best known of these startups was People Express, founded by Donald Burr, formerly of Texas International, which consistently undercut the major players on a variety of popular routes.

But these new, smaller airlines were not only start-up companies run by eager entrepreneurs. Deregulation and the return to something resembling free-market competition led top managers of the major airlines to begin cutting their own throats. The large players in the industry set up non-union subsidiaries to compete with other major carriers in certain key markets. New York Air, for example, was formed by Texas International to compete with Eastern flights out of La Guardia airport in New York.

Al Brescia, a vice president at Eastern, summed up the situation that airline management found themselves in when faced with the abrupt switch from a regulated oligopoly: "We were thrown to the wolves . . . but we were the wolves and the chickens all at the same time, and we were all looking for a free lunch. We've learned there is no free lunch" (Sampson 1984, 136).

These "low cost" airlines had only captured 8 percent of the market by 1983. But their impact was felt in much more dramatic terms by the "fare wars" they set off. The major players in the industry were forced for the first time to compete and thereby to offer reduced fares. The first major casualty of airline deregulation was Braniff Airways. Braniff had been around since the 1920s, yet deregulation took its toll on the company. In the following well-publicized, recorded telephone exchange, Robert Crandall, president of American Airlines, and Howard Putnam, chairman of Braniff, discussed the beating the two companies were taking through competition on fares:

> *Putnam:* Do you have a suggestion for me?
>
> *Crandall:* Yes, I have a suggestion for you. Raise your goddamn fares 20%. I'll raise mine the next morning.
>
> *Putnam:* Robert, we . . .

Crandall: You'll make money and I will too.

Putnam: We can't talk about pricing.

Crandall: Oh [expletive], Howard. We can talk about any goddamn thing we want to talk about.[2]

The ramifications of airline deregulation were to be far-reaching. Consumers were soon to benefit from reduced fares, at least on the most popular routes.[3] But, the cozy, stable relationship between airlines and their employees was also about to end. Deregulation brought more pressures on airlines to cut fares and compete. In the airline industry, costs such as fuel and labor are a substantial component of operating expenses. As a result, profit levels are highly sensitive to changes in these costs.

More important, costs in the airline industry do not vary proportionately with the level of passenger traffic. To give a simple example, if a jet flies with 25 passengers or 200, many of the cost factors, such as fuel and labor, remain the same. You still use roughly the same amount of fuel, you still need a pilot, copilot, flight engineer, and so on. You need supply fewer peanuts to 25 people than to 200, but this is not a major component of airline costs. Profit levels, therefore, are extremely sensitive to changes in passenger traffic and in fares (which can rapidly shift passenger traffic).

In the 1970s, airlines greatly overestimated the growth in air traffic and purchased too many planes. The industry as a whole was faced with overcapacity. This in turn led to new pressures to cut fares in order to attract passengers to offset

2. This conversation became the basis of a Justice Department charge of price-fixing. See Sampson 1984, 139–41.

3. According to economic models, deregulation should reduce rates. However, in the airline industry rates have *risen* since deregulation, although at a slower rate than the consumer price index. Deregulation tends to lead to higher rates on less popular routes, or eliminate those routes altogether. Similarly, if postal service was not "regulated" by the government, the price of stamps might rise less rapidly, but there might be no one willing to take letters to certain remote destinations.

the fixed costs mentioned above. This overcapacity coincided with deregulation and the accompanying incentives to cut fares.

All of these factors led to great pressures to reduce costs. Airline stock prices languished in the years after deregulation, and edgy creditors stepped up pressure on the airlines to cut costs (Sampson 1984).

THE EMERGENCE OF FRANK LORENZO

Frank Lorenzo, the son of a hairdresser who emigrated from Spain and settled in Queens, New York, graduated from Columbia University in 1961 and Harvard Business School in 1963. In popular accounts of Lorenzo's childhood, we are told that he enjoyed reading the biographies of men like Andrew Carnegie (*NYT*, December 30, 1984, sec. 3:6). His first taste of the airline industry occurred when he became a financial analyst for TWA. He later worked as a financial planning manager at Eastern. But Lorenzo yearned to run his own airline.

In 1966, Lorenzo and a Harvard Business School classmate, Robert Carney, invested $1,000 in a firm they aptly called the Lorenzo Carney Company. The company was formed to provide financial consulting to the airline industry. Three years later, in 1969, the two partners formed Jet Capital. Ostensibly, Jet was to enter the aircraft-leasing business, but in reality Jet was a shell for Lorenzo and Carney to raise money from the financial markets based on the two partners' financial expertise in the airline industry.

In 1972, six years before airline deregulation, Jet used the money it had raised from venture capitalists to take control of Texas International Airlines, a debt-laden regional carrier based in the Southwest. As part of the acquisition plan, Jet reached an agreement with its financial backers to restrict and restructure TI's debt. Texas International's chief lender was Chase Manhattan Bank, and Chase clearly wanted new management for TI in order to salvage its outstanding loans to the airline (Murphy 1986, 14). Chase Manhattan backed Jet's takeover of TI because it thought that Lorenzo and Carney would act to put TI on a sound financial footing. Lorenzo and Carney immediately cut unprofitable routes and raised some fares, and by 1973 the company even made a small profit. However, over the next eight years, TI's financial results were inconsistent.[4]

While heading Texas International in the early 1970s, Lorenzo experienced a taste of the deregulated world that all airlines would soon find themselves in. Texas International competed against a small carrier called Southwest Airlines. Because Southwest was an intra-state carrier (it only flew in Texas), it was exempt from CAB regulations, including the regulated fare structure. This created for Texas International, with most of its own flights in Texas, a microcosm of the deregulated world that would arrive in the airline industry as a whole in 1978. TI was forced to compete against an airline that could offer rock-bottom fares.

Lorenzo's reaction to this competitive situation was to get the CAB to approve the introduction of half-price, off-peak fares—called "peanut fares" in the regulated industry ("peanut" referred not only to the low cost but also to the fact that passengers were given a bag of peanuts rather than a full meal on these flights). TI's application to the CAB for "peanut fares" was a highly unusual move during those times of strict regulation (*Fortune*, January 9, 1984, 66), and it earned Lorenzo a reputation as a fare and cost cutter. According to many in the industry, Lorenzo was held in high esteem at the CAB as "commit[ted] to low fares" while others in the industry referred to Lorenzo as "the embodiment of deregulation" (Murphy 1986, 23). Much to the surprise of many managers at the major airlines, Lorenzo received CAB approval to introduce peanut fares, which helped TI com-

---

4. Profits climbed through 1978, then fell with deregulation. By 1981, TI reported a net loss.

pete with Southwest. But peanut fares led in turn to more pressure to reduce costs as the airline oligopoly began to crumble.

In Lorenzo's quest to keep profits rising, Texas International attempted to acquire National Airlines in 1978, but after buying up National stock, TI was finally outbid by Pan Am. However, TI made a profit of $47 million when it gave up on its takeover attempt and finally sold its stock in National. Next, Lorenzo and Carney reorganized TI into a holding company called Texas Air Corp.

Despite the sizable profit from the sale of National stock, Lorenzo still needed to cut costs in order to continue his peanut fares. In 1980, Texas Air started New York Air and invited the former CAB chairman Arthur Kahn, who had engineered airline deregulation, to join the board of directors of New York Air. This low-cost, non-union airline was formed to compete with unionized air carriers on the busy New York–Washington and New York–Boston routes. At New York Air, pilots were paid approximately one-half the salary paid to pilots at unionized carriers. Airline unions were outraged and viewed Lorenzo as a threat to unions in the industry as a whole.

Lorenzo rose to prominence not through his expertise in aviation but through his financial expertise as applied to the industry. He continued building his reputation in financial circles because of his ability to deal with deregulation—namely, to cut costs in the newly competitive era. In retrospect, he seemed ideally suited to the emerging world of deregulation in the airline industry. Robert Six, with his background in engineering and aviation, headed Continental during the days of regulation. Lorenzo, with his background in finance and his experience as a cost cutter, would soon rise to lead Continental through deregulation.

LORENZO TAKES OVER CONTINENTAL

In late 1979, Robert Six retired as CEO of Continental and picked Alvin Feldman as his successor. Six remained as chairman of the board. Feldman, a mechanical engineer who had worked for General Dynamics, Aerojet General, and Frontier Airlines, also apparently enjoyed good relations with employees at Continental (Murphy 1986, 10–13).

Continental began to initiate a long-term "dual hub" strategy: using both Denver and Houston as hubs for its other air routes. However, United Airlines, a much bigger company than Continental, also decided to build a Denver hub. United's decision eroded much of the competitive advantage Continental hoped to reap from its Denver hub.

Meanwhile, Frank Lorenzo was continuing to look for acquisition candidates. After his attempted takeover of National, Lorenzo made another unsuccessful play, this time for TWA, an airline eleven times the size of TI. Then, in 1980, Lorenzo hired two investment advisors, Smith Barney, Harris Upham & Co. and Kidder, Peabody, to prepare reports on a possible takeover of Continental. Kidder, Peabody reported that institutional investors held over 30 percent of the stock in Continental and outlined a strategy for acquiring these shares as a foundation for a complete takeover of the company (Murphy 1986, 22). The investment advisors argued that the high percentage of institutional holdings would make Continental an easier takeover target than a company with widely dispersed stock. Lorenzo need only secure a deal with a few institutions to gain effective control of Continental.

Smith Barney helped arrange for TI to acquire approximately 800,000, or 9.5 percent, of Continental's shares in just two major transactions (Murphy 1986, 25). In February 1980, TI announced its intention to acquire an additional six million Continental shares from Continental shareholders, which would have raised its stake to 80 percent. TI had arranged a loan commitment from Manufacturers Hanover Trust, totaling $50 million, to help finance the takeover.

Continental's management began a campaign to thwart the takeover. They hired the financial relations firm Georgeson & Company to contact institutional investors in an attempt to dissuade them from selling to Lorenzo and TI.

Georgeson found it rough going, however, as institutional investors argued that their fiduciary responsibility required them to take the higher stock price from TI. This, however, apparently did not prevent at least a few institutions from siding with Continental's management. Continental did much better with individual shareholders, many of whom reportedly expressed anti-Lorenzo feelings (Murphy 1986, 32).

But because of the high percentage of institutional investment in Continental, TI was able to purchase 49 percent of Continental by mid-March. Continental desperately searched for a "white knight" to provide a friendly takeover, but was unsuccessful, since few companies wanted to move into the airline industry during this time of deregulation and declining profits unless there was a clear strategy to reduce costs. Continental also tried to get the emasculated CAB to intervene in the takeover. But, the CAB was now pushing for deregulation and argued that the "free market" required it to allow shareholders the option of voting on the takeover.

Continental's unions feared the takeover. Lorenzo had had a strong anti-union reputation since he had begun New York Air, and TI had already announced that it would try to renegotiate all labor contracts at Continental after the takeover. In an attempt to keep the airline away from TI, Continental's employees pursued their own effort to acquire the company through an Employee Stock Ownership Plan (ESOP). The ESOP gained the approval of most of Continental's top managers, who were becoming desperate in their attempt to stave off the unfriendly bid.

However, Continental's lead creditor, Chase Manhattan Bank, opposed the effort by the employees to buy the company, apparently preferring Lorenzo's cost-cutting strategy to the ESOP. Lorenzo had enjoyed good relations with financial creditors over the years. An official close to Texas Air said, "[Lorenzo] always has his finger on the pulse of the money markets," and that he should have no trouble finding "people willing to put out a lot of money for a play in an airline" (*Wall Street Journal* [hereafter cited as *WSJ*], October 14, 1983, 3).

Texas International argued strongly against the idea of an ESOP, advancing the argument to financial analysts and holders of Continental stock that an ESOP would lead to uncontrolled wage demands. A Kidder, Peabody report supported TI's position: "In my opinion, however, the employees—many of whom are represented by unions—would have a strong incentive . . . to seek to boost their wages" (Murphy 1986, 93). There was little evidence to back up this assertion, since there had been relatively little experience with ESOPs in the United States at the time. The argument being made by the financial analysts and TI, and apparently accepted by Chase Manhattan, rested on an assumption that the employees would run their own company into the ground. Many in the financial community simply ruled out the idea of employee ownership, preferring Lorenzo's anti-union cost-cutting strategy. Chase Manhattan decided to support Lorenzo's effort and not to support the ESOP. When other financial institutions followed Chase's lead, the ESOP effort failed owing to lack of financial support.

By June of 1982, Lorenzo and TI had gained control of Continental after a bitter battle that had lasted close to three years. Frank Lorenzo became the CEO of Continental and merged Texas International Airlines Inc. and Continental Air Lines Inc. into the Continental Airlines Corporation.

LABOR TROUBLE AND PRE-BANKRUPTCY MANEUVERS

Lorenzo's plan for Continental was to "provide all of the frills of flying but at discounted fares" (*Fortune*, January 9, 1984, 66–73). Specifically, Lorenzo hoped to provide in-flight movies, meals, and drinks like the major airlines, but with cheaper fares. Clearly, the only way to do this would be to reduce costs well below those of other competitors that provided these frills. Lorenzo said he wanted to reduce Continental's labor costs from 35 to 25 percent of the company's $1.5 billion operating budget (*NYT*, September 26, 1983, D1).

Very shortly after taking over Continental, Lorenzo imposed a 15 percent wage cut on its non-union employees, achieving $30 million in labor savings. Lorenzo sought an additional $100 million in labor savings from the pilots and the flight attendants. Both of these groups, however, were unionized and resisted concessions.

During a meeting in June 1983, Richard Adams, Continental's senior vice president for flight operations, jotted down some handwritten notes that would come back to haunt him in the following years: "I don't believe we can get these concessions on a voluntary, persuasive basis. We must get [an] awfully big stick. . . . Most effective stick might be Chapter 11" (court testimony, *In re* Continental Airlines, 3 Bankr. L. Rep. [CCH] [Bankr. S. D. Tex. 1984], and Murphy 1984, 223). And in the same set of notes, Adams said of the pilot union's chief negotiator, Larry Baxter: "[We might try to] change Baxter['s] position, or get Baxter overridden—which may mean overthrown."

It was clear that three months before Continental eventually filed for bankruptcy, at least one top management member saw Chapter 11 as a strategic "stick" to defeat the labor unions and to gain wage concessions (*Aviation Week and Space Technology*, October 10, 1983, 32). Later—in bankruptcy court—the unions would claim that this was the "smoking gun" that proved that Continental was not truly bankrupt, and that management considered Chapter 11 a means to negate collective bargaining agreements and impose wage cuts.

During this period, Continental was negotiating with the International Association of Machinists (IAM), which represented Continental's 2,100 mechanics. The IAM had just completed a successful contract negotiation with Eastern, achieving wage increases of 32 percent over three years and was expecting comparable concessions from Lorenzo (Murphy 1986, 231). The negotiations became extremely bitter on both sides when Continental adopted the strategy of *reducing* its offer to the mechanics as the negotiations proceeded (*Business Week,* November 7, 1983, 111–15). Although Continental stated that it followed this bizarre bargaining strategy because the company's financial situation was worsening by the day, the IAM charged that Lorenzo was trying to ensure a strike in order to replace union mechanics with non-union employees.

The mechanics voted to strike in August 1983. On August 16, Continental began replacing many of the 2,100 mechanics with non-union mechanics, paying the replacements approximately 67 percent of what the unionized mechanics were earning. At the same time, Continental management asked for over $100 million in concessions from Continental's other employee groups and gave them until September 14 to respond to the demand. During a September meeting with the pilots' union, Lorenzo indicated that if concessions were not accepted, Continental might consider "actions to protect our liquidity and other resources." When asked what these actions might be, Lorenzo reportedly told the pilots, "Something you may not like" (quoted in Murphy 1986, 241). It was clear to all that Lorenzo was threatening to put the company into Chapter 11 bankruptcy.

On September 21, Continental's president, Stephen Wolf, resigned because he wanted to continue trying to reach an accommodation with the unions. Though this appeared cryptic at the time, his resignation came just three days before the bankruptcy filing, indicating that he opposed the move that Continental was about to make. Days before the filing in bankruptcy court, Frank Lorenzo assumed the roles of both president and chief executive officer of Continental.

CONTINENTAL FILES FOR CHAPTER 11

On September 24, 1983, Continental Airlines filed for Chapter 11 bankruptcy. Lorenzo was quoted in a *New York Times* article published two days after the filing as saying: "It wasn't a problem of cash. Our sole problem was labor." Continental's unions would use this statement (probably made to placate edgy creditors) in their argument that Continental's bankruptcy was a strategic maneuver to wrest concessions from the unions.

Immediately upon filing, Continental suspended all of its flights. Three days later, however, Continental resumed half of those flights, using only one-third of its employees and paying some of them only half their normal wages. Thus, Continental unilaterally abrogated its collective bargaining agreements with its various unions, imposing wage cuts of up to 50 percent on employees returning to work after the bankruptcy. The company also instituted new work rules intended to cut operating expenses by a further 25 percent. These new rules included longer stretches of work, no guaranteed periods of time off, and shorter rest breaks.

Frank Lorenzo began referring to the company as the "new Continental" and to any employee working for the company after the bankruptcy petition as a "founding employee" (see Continental Airlines, annual report, 1983). One employee of the "new Continental" had his salary reduced from $45,000 to $30,000 and his title reduced from copilot to flight engineer (*NYT*, September 24, 1984, D1). The average captain's compensation declined from $87,000 per year before the bankruptcy to $43,000 after the filing. Some ticket agents who earned $10 per hour before the bankruptcy had their wages cut to $7.50 per hour after the filing (*NYT*, September 6, 1985, D2). Through bankruptcy, Lorenzo imposed the wage concessions he had been unsuccessfully trying to obtain through the collective bargaining process.

To be sure, Continental had been losing money in the years since deregulation. The airline experienced a total loss of $500 million between 1978 and the 1983 filing, but the airline industry as a whole had also lost money in 1981, 1982, and 1983 (*NYT*, November 20, 1988, sec. 3:1). Filing for Chapter 11 bankruptcy was not precipitated by a cash crisis, as Lorenzo admitted; at the time of the filing, Continental, the nation's eighth largest carrier, still had cash and marketable securities amounting to about $58 million, $186 million in general accounts receivable, and $44 million in accounts receivable from Continental affiliates, as well as sizable assets that it could have converted into cash. Continental could have chosen to continue without Chapter 11 protection. It might have continued to lose money, or it might have reached some accommodation with its unions, or Lorenzo might have found some other cost-cutting or revenue-raising strategy.

Continental had also engaged in several actions just prior to bankruptcy that led the airline's unions to charge that the bankruptcy was intended to break the unions. In July, one month before the IAM strike, Continental had reportedly hired bankruptcy specialists at the New York law firm Weil, Gotschal & Manges to begin serious consideration of a Chapter 11 bankruptcy (see Murphy 1986, 239–41). In addition, the company had moved assets around to pave the way for the bankruptcy filing. Just prior to declaring Chapter 11, Continental shifted its international flights to three new subsidiaries, which were then excluded from the filing.

Continental also excluded its parent, Texas Air, from the bankruptcy filing. On September 15, just a week before the filing, Continental publicly offered 2.5 million common shares, thereby reducing Texas Air's holdings in Continental and helping to validate the claim that the two companies were separate entities. This move would later help substantiate Continental's claim that it did business "at arm's length" from Texas Air. If Texas Air's resources had been included as part of Continental, it might have led to the dismissal of any claim to bankruptcy. Continental argued in court, however, that the two companies (Continental and Texas Air) had always done business "at arm's length," thereby meeting the legal test for considering Continental an independent entity able to declare Chapter 11 based on its own balance sheet.

The unions and commercial creditors argued against the exclusion of Texas Air from the bankruptcy proceeding. Both of these groups stood to gain by the inclusion of the parent company, since they each could make claims upon the resources of both the parent and Continental. The unions and creditors argued that Texas Air owned 90 percent of Continental and that several transactions between the two indicated that business was not always "at arm's length." Continental had sold $7.75 million in bonds to Texas Air in June 1983. "This sticks out as more than just a nice gesture," one of the creditors commented sarcastically (*WSJ*, October 26, 1983, 12).

The unions also questioned several asset swaps between Continental and Texas Air. The most embarrassing of these for Continental was the acquisition by non-union New York Air (also owned by Texas Air) of landing rights to three gates at National Airport in Washington, D.C. New York Air agreed to purchase these rights from Continental for $757,000. But, as Continental admitted in court, New York Air never paid Continental the money. Continental's legal counsel admitted the details of the incident but argued against the general conclusion that Continental and Texas Air were trying to move assets from unionized Continental to non-union New York Air (see *In re* Continental Airlines, 3 Bankr. L. Rep. [CCH] [Bankr. S.D. Tex. 1984]).

The unions questioned other transactions as well. Continental had bought Texas Air's pilot-training facility, sending $5.9 million to the parent company, thereby worsening the company's financial condition on paper. The union argued that this was another attempt to move liquid assets to the parent. Texas Air acquired Continental's computer services unit for $15 million, which the union charged grossly undervalued the unit, saying that it could have been sold for much more.

The power to designate the "bankrupt unit" and the ability to move assets among subsidiaries can lead to crucial differences in the determination of whether bankruptcy proceedings can go forward. The federal bankruptcy code has no requirement that a debtor be insolvent. But bankruptcy courts have the power to dismiss Chapter 11 proceedings for "cause" (11 U.S.C. § 1112b [1979]). One such cause might be the solvency of the debtor, and so insolvency is nevertheless an important goal for any debtor considering bankruptcy. Insolvency is based on a ratio between assets and liabilities (11 U.S.C. § 101 [26] [1979]). But, exactly which assets do we count? This becomes an absolutely crucial question in cases where bankruptcy is pursued as strategy. It is clear that there is fairly wide leeway in the way in which this seemingly technical concept can be manipulated.

Continental's unions also argued that Continental could have gotten additional capital from Texas Air in order to keep flying. Interestingly, Barry Simon, Continental's legal counsel, responded that this was not considered since "the banks would have rejected the idea" (*WSJ*, December 5, 1983, 5). Simon indicated that Continental's creditors would not have been happy had the company failed to cut labor costs and borrowed more money from Texas Air. The firm could also have borrowed additional money from creditors, but apparently was refused further loans unless it gained labor concessions. This implies that the "cost of money" is not as amenable to reduction as the cost of labor. Simon's comment, quoted above, indicates that the firm might have tried to borrow more money, but that the banks stood firm in demanding reductions in the cost of labor.

Despite these examples of moving assets among Continental, Texas Air, and other affiliates, the bankruptcy court judge supported Continental's claim that business was at arm's length and allowed the filing of the Chapter 11 petition.

Although Continental's unions and bank creditors joined together to argue that Texas Air's assets should have been included in the bankruptcy filing, the two split on the issue of whether Continental should be in Chapter 11 at all. It is clear why the unions and creditors both wanted Texas Air included in the filing: more assets would be available for the claims of both workers and lenders. It is not exactly clear, however, why the lenders did not side with the unions on the question of whether Continental was indeed bankrupt. Often, lenders are assumed to be against early voluntary bankruptcy filings, since all loan payments are stayed during the proceeding (the filing immediately allowed Continental to halt payments on its $650 million in outstanding loans). It seems that the lenders understood Continental's strategy of declaring Chapter 11 in order to reduce labor costs and judged the gamble of bankruptcy to be in their best interests as well. They might have reckoned that this strategy would work, and that they would then stand a better chance of recovering all of their loan capital through a reorganization based on a reduction in labor costs. In fact, Lorenzo told the creditors soon after the filing that "[creditors] can expect to do very well" (*WSJ*, September 26, 1983, 1).

The unions' attempt to have the bankruptcy filing thrown out on "bad faith" grounds (i.e., that the firm was not really bankrupt) failed. On January 17, 1984, the bankruptcy court rejected the unions' petition to have the bankruptcy filing dismissed.

Continental's unions, along with labor experts around the country, reacted vehemently to the bankruptcy filing (*Aviation Week and Space Technology*, October 10, 1983, 32). Vern Countryman, a Harvard law professor and bankruptcy expert, stated: "If their sole purpose is to get rid of collective bargaining contracts, then it's a misuse of the Chapter [11] and courts won't allow them to do it" (*WSJ*, September 26, 1983, 1). Shortly after the filing, the Air Line Pilots Association and the Union of Flight Attendants joined the already-striking International Association of Machinists on the picket line. Continental thus had its three main groups of unionized employees—pilots, flight attendants, and mechanics—on strike against the company.

THE CRUCIAL FIRST WEEK

Continental had obviously taken a large risk putting itself into Chapter 11 bankruptcy, particularly since it counted on consumers to continue buying tickets after its announcement. Continental had learned from Braniff's bankruptcy experience in 1982 that it needed to assure the flying public immediately that it was still a viable, ongoing enterprise despite declaring bankruptcy.

The airline quickly hired strikebreakers to replace unionized machinists, pilots, and flight attendants. Continental also got a few members of each group to cross the picket line and work for the "new Continental." It gradually increased the number of flights it offered in the days following the bankruptcy filing.

But Continental knew that customers would shy away if they feared they might be stuck with the worthless tickets of a bankrupt company. In an effort to quell such fears, the airline undertook a bold maneuver just days after the filing, announcing a $49 fare on ALL nonstop flights in the United States. The $49 fare, ridiculously low for cross-continental flights, would be in effect for one week, followed by a $79 fare for two more weeks.

Continental's low fare received tremendous publicity, and customers began to line up at airports for the cheap flights. Douglas Birdsall, Continental's vice president for market planning, said at the time, "You can buy the back page of the newspaper anytime you want. But $49 for a ticket from Denver to New York gets you on the front page for free" (*Fortune*, January 9, 1984, 66). This low fare gave Continental not only publicity, but also credibility, inducing consumers to take the chance of flying with the airline. In addition, anecdotal evidence suggests that the public was willing to accept the company's definition of the situation: that it was in bankruptcy but not really broke. The reduction in the stigma attached to bankruptcy that I outlined in chapter 1 thus had very real implications. If people were willing to accept the company's definition of the meaning of the bankruptcy, they would continue to support the company through ticket purchases, making Continental better able to survive the bankruptcy process intact.

How was a "bankrupt" company able to offer fares that were far cheaper than those of any other airline? Part of the answer, of course, lay in the fact that Continental had just reduced its labor costs by 50 percent by unilaterally breaking collective bargaining agreements. But the rest of the answer lies in the fact that Continental chose to declare bankruptcy early enough to have substantial liquid assets to carry it through those first few weeks. Continental, in effect, had a $58 million cushion to play with, which allowed the airline to hire back 4,000 of its 12,000 employees, along with new pilots. Continental also persuaded the bankruptcy court to free up $40 million in restricted cash and to substitute new receivables as collateral. This helped Continental to keep flying during those early weeks. Instead of a tame, bankrupt airline, Continental acted during the first few weeks after filing for bankruptcy like a fierce, fare-slashing competitor.

The importance of Continental's ability to keep flying and cut fares to attract customers in those first few days of bankruptcy cannot be stressed too strongly. Continental's lenders were watching very carefully in order to determine whether to support the company's voluntary bankruptcy filing, oppose the filing on the grounds that the company was not really bankrupt, or push for a liquidation of the company in order to garner as much of the company's assets as possible before further deterioration or losses. After the first day of the "new Continental," an unidentified secured creditor was quoted as saying, "If things don't improve dramatically within a week, we will go to court to prevent Continental from continuing to fly" (*WSJ*, September 29, 1983, 2). A lawyer representing an insurance company, American General, one of Continental's largest secured creditors, indicated the strategy commercial creditors were following: "My guess is that the [secured] creditors will allow Continental to operate until they deplete the cash on hand" (ibid.). So Continental had just a few days to show the creditors that its strategy would work.

As Continental managed to woo passengers during the first crucial days of its bankruptcy, the lenders supported its request to use $40 million in cash as operating capital and replace this liquid capital with new receivables (not yet collected) as collateral. This $40 million in liquid capital would normally have been restricted by the court to cover pre-bankruptcy debt (including the debt owed to the lenders). However, the lenders made the decision to join Continental's strategic gamble. In an eleventh-hour agreement, pounded out just minutes before a hearing in the bankruptcy court, Continental's major banks, led by Chase Manhattan, agreed to support the airline's request for the freeing up of the additional funds (*WSJ*, November 23, 1983, 3). Continental used the money to subsidize its $49 fare.

Continental's competitors also closely watched the first few weeks unfold, but they were, however, in a bind. Continental had dramatically altered its cost structure, reducing labor costs by 50 percent in one fell swoop, which enabled it to cut fares dramatically. Competing airlines could match those fares, but only at substantial losses, since they continued to operate with much higher cost structures.

The competition responded swiftly with their own cost-cutting efforts. Two weeks after Continental's Chapter 11 filing, American Airlines instituted a two-tier wage scale for its pilots. New pilots at American would henceforth earn 50 percent of what new pilots had previously earned. Three days later, Delta imposed a wage freeze on its 32,000 non-union employees (Neilson 1984, 385). While these actions were considerably less drastic than Continental's wage cuts, they were the beginning of an adjustment triggered by Continental's actions.

Industry analysts feared major fare wars. Eliot Fried, an airline analyst at Shearson/American Express, commented, "Every airline continues to monitor Continental's progress. If any carrier believes that Continental is increasing their market share substantially, they will react" (*NYT*, January 18, 1984, D1). United, for example, matched some of Continental's fares, seeking to "limit" its response to Continental (*NYT*, February 17, 1984, D3). Evidently Continental's competitors were willing to concede increased profits to Continental (i.e., with very low costs, Continental could conceivably make larger profits than the competition) but would not tolerate any loss in *market share*.[5] United and others selectively matched Continental's low fares on routes where they saw Continental increasing its market share at their expense.

The competition was clearly worried about Continental, realizing that Lorenzo was serious about his attempt to provide "all the frills of flying at discount fares." Richard Ferris, the CEO of United Airlines, was asked a question about low-cost, non-union People Express during a Wall Street meeting of security analysts. Although the questioner asked about People Express, Ferris answered: "I'm more worried about Continental than People Express" (*NYT*, December 30, 1984, sec. 3:6).

Several airline executives indicated that Continental's bankruptcy might lead to more planned bankruptcies among airlines forced to compete with Continental. Frank Borman, asked whether he might take Eastern Air Lines into Chapter 11 to reduce labor costs, replied, "We're seeing that tested right now" (*WSJ*, January 18, 1984, 2). An unnamed official at Texas Air told the *Wall Street Journal* (September 26, 1983, 1) that "this filing might start a trend. It may become almost 'in' to say, 'We're under court protection, are you?'" William Smith, Eastern's sales manager, said more pointedly, "[Continental] is becoming a real threat to the cost structure of some airlines" (*WSJ*, January 27, 1984, 8). Julius Maldutis, an airline analyst at Salomon Brothers, said, "[The wage gap] has given Continental a jump. The other carriers are

5. Oligopolistic markets are often characterized by this sort of behavior (see Baran and Sweezy 1966). Oligopolistic firms will meet reduced prices when there is a threat to market share. Major airlines, long used to operating under oligopolistic competition, had presumably learned well the lessons of "corespective behavior" (Schumpeter 1950, 90).

gradually moving in the direction of a two-tiered wage structure. They will get there, but it will take a couple of years" (*NYT*, August 1, 1984, D3).

THE CLASH BETWEEN BANKRUPTCY LAW AND LABOR LAW

Section 8(d) of the National Labor Relations Act (NLRA) forbids an employer to terminate or modify the terms of a collective bargaining agreement prior to the expiration of the contract without the agreement of the union. Any unilateral modification of a mandatory bargaining term (wages, working conditions, etc.) is an unfair labor practice (Roberts 1987, 1018). Continental's unions charged that the company's unilateral violation of its labor contracts violated the National Labor Relations Act and, by extension, the National Railway Act.

However, the bankruptcy code permits the rejection of executory contracts. An executory contract is "a contract under which the obligation of both the bankrupt and the other party to the contract are so underperformed that the failure of either party to complete performance would constitute a material breach excusing the performance of the other" (Countryman 1973, 439). Stated more simply for the purpose at hand, an executory contract is one that has not yet been fulfilled.

The rejection of executory contracts in bankruptcy is allowed under sections 365(a) and 1107(a) of the 1978 Bankruptcy Code, but the right goes back at least as far as England's Bankruptcy Act of 1869. The U.S. Bankruptcy Act of 1898 incorporated this right from the English law in section 313 (1), which permitted the rejection of executory contracts (see Zurofsky 1987).

Bankruptcy law has allowed the rejection of such contracts as rental agreements based on a "simple business judgment" standard: (a) Is the contract executory? (b) Would it benefit the debtor to reject the contract? If both tests are met, rejection is normally allowed (see Borman's Inc. v. Allied Supermarket, 706 F.2d 187, 189 [6th Cir. 1983], *cert. denied*, 104 S. Ct. 263 [1983]).

However, since the Bankruptcy Act of 1841, wages have been treated differently from other types of debts. The rationale for treating wages differently was that "the working man and his family [*sic*] depended upon this single source of payment, whereas other creditors, who were in business, had a number of different customers and were not so reliant upon payment from a single origin" (Merrick 1986, 187). So because a worker counts solely on a wage to survive, courts have tended to treat labor contracts differently from other executory business contracts.

A collective bargaining agreement is very different from other executory contracts in that a collective bargaining agreement normally contains rights, bargained for by employees, that cannot be easily reduced to monetary terms: seniority procedures, grievance procedures, rules governing scope and conditions of work, meal periods, discipline procedures, no strike and no lockout clauses, and so forth. Since these rights are also destroyed when the agreement is rejected, a claim for monetary damages for a breach of the agreement would not end up compensating employees for these rights (see Bordewieck and Countryman 1983, 312).

At a more fundamental level, court-approved rejection of a collective bargaining agreement allows the debtor to commit what would be the most flagrantly unfair labor practice if it were to occur outside of the bankruptcy context. There is some conflict, then, between labor law and bankruptcy law. This sort of conflict is not unusual in the legal arena, and it is often in these legal interstices that social policy ends up being made by the court.

The main legal issues in the case thus boiled down to these questions:

1. Were Continental's union contracts executory and therefore subject to rejection?

2. If so, what should be the standard for allowing rejection of a collective bargaining agreement.

3. Could Continental unilaterally reject its collective bargaining agreements without first getting the approval of the bankruptcy court?

There was little or no debate on the first issue. The collective bargaining agreements in force at Continental were clearly executory contracts. The main issue, therefore, was the standard to be applied in allowing or disallowing rejection. Fairly well developed case law in this area provided precedents for the Continental case. Perhaps the first important case to be decided by the courts was that of Kevin Steel (Shopmen's Local Union No. 455 v. Kevin Steel Products, 519 F.2d 698 [2d Cir. 1975]). In the original case, the court ruled that Kevin Steel could reject its labor contract because a company in bankruptcy was in fact a "new entity," a different company from the one that had declared bankruptcy. Based on this legal fiction, the "new entity" was not bound by the past labor contract (this "new entity" theory, however, was not supported in a later Supreme Court ruling in a subsequent case [see NLRB v. Bildisco & Bildisco 465 U.S. 513 (1984); Haydel 1984]).

On appeal, the Second Circuit court decided that collective bargaining agreements may indeed be rejected, but under a more stringent standard than the simple "business judgment" test. The court decision clearly reflected the conflict between bankruptcy law and labor law:

> The decision to allow rejection should not be based solely on whether it will improve the financial status of the debtor. Such a narrow approach totally ignores the policies of the Labor Act . . . a bankruptcy court should permit rejection of a collective bargaining agreement only after thorough scrutiny and a careful balancing of the equities on both sides, for, in relieving the debtor from its obligations under a collective bargaining agreement, it may be depriving employees affected of their seniority, welfare and pension rights. . . . That

would leave the employees without compensation for their
losses . . . enabling the debtor, at the expense of the employees, to consummate what may be a more favorable plan of
arrangement with its other creditors and the bankruptcy
court must move cautiously in allowing rejection of a collective bargaining agreement. (Shopmen's Local Union No. 455
v. Kevin Steel Products, 519 F.2d 707 [2d Cir. 1975])

So Kevin Steel required a "balancing of the equities"
when considering the rejection of a union contract. This
phrase was almost hopelessly vague and left it up to future
courts to interpret it. At least one legal commentator has
called the "balancing of the equities" test "a subjective exercise not susceptible to precise quantification or qualification" (Miller 1984, 1125–26). This test has generally been
construed to mean that all parties to the bankruptcy should
suffer to some "similar," but again undefined, degree. *Similar* did not necessarily mean equal.

Despite being vague, the decision did set a precedent that
labor contracts were in some way different from other business contracts. Several months later, the court adopted a
more stringent standard for rejection in Brotherhood of Railway, Airline, and Steamship Clerks v. REA Express (523 F.2d
164 172 [2d Cir.], *cert. denied*, 423 U.S. 1017 [1975]). "In view
of the serious effects which rejection has on the employees,
[rejection] should be authorized only where it clearly appears to be the lesser of two evils and that unless the agreement is rejected [the debtor] will collapse and the employees
will no longer have their jobs," the court decided in that
case, breaking away from a simple balancing of equities.

Under the REA Express test, collective bargaining agreements could only be rejected when the employees would be
likely to lose their jobs entirely through the collapse of the
company (see Balin 1983). The next major case to be decided,
Alan Wood Steel (*In re* Alan Wood Steel Co., 449 F. Supp.
165 [E.D.Pa. 1978]), made the standard for rejection even a
bit tougher, requiring a two-step test: (1) rejection was allowed only if it appeared the debtor would collapse without

rejection (the REA Express test), (2) a balancing of the equities favoring rejection (the Kevin Steel test). The Alan Wood test was even more demanding because it required that the debtor meet *both* tests. Thus, the rejection of a labor contract could be disallowed *even if* it meant the collapse of the debtor. For example, consider a case where, although management salaries were grossly out of line with the pay of the employees, management wished to cut the employees' pay to the bone, while giving managers massive raises as a result. In this case, the court might decide that failing to reject the union contract might mean the collapse of the debtor, but the balancing of the equities might still prevent rejection of the union contract.

The general legal trend through the 1970s was thus to enforce more stringent tests for allowing companies to reject their union contracts. This, however, conflicted with the trend in bankruptcy law detailed in chapter 1; namely, broadening bankruptcy relief in order to keep businesses solvent.

The Supreme Court still had not ruled on the crucial issues pertaining to the unilateral rejection of labor contracts. But thousands of miles away from Continental's Texas headquarters, a small New Jersey building concern had declared bankruptcy and voided its union contract. The case of the Bildisco Manufacturing Company had been accepted for review by the Supreme Court and was soon scheduled for a hearing. Both the management of Continental and union leaders were watching the Bildisco case very carefully.

THE BILDISCO CASE

In April 1979, Bildisco signed a three-year contract with Teamsters Local 408, which represented 45 percent of Bildisco's work force (numbering under 100 at the time). In January 1980, Bildisco failed to pay health and pension benefits called for in the contract and failed to remit union dues collected from paychecks, effectively breaking the labor contract. Sal Valente, president of Bildisco, testified in the original bankruptcy case that the small company's creditors had told him that they were worried about "the union situation" (Browning 1984, 60). Three months later, the firm filed for Chapter 11 bankruptcy, and soon thereafter it gained court approval of its rejection of the labor agreement. The union filed an unfair labor practice charge with the NLRB. The NLRB agreed with the union and would pursue the case to the Supreme Court. Bankruptcy law and labor law were at odds.

The Supreme Court eventually agreed to hear the Bildisco case, brought on a joint appeal by the National Labor Relations Board and the Teamsters. The two issues faced by the Court were similar to the issues in the Continental case: (1) What standard should be used for the rejection of collective bargaining contracts? and (2) Can a company unilaterally reject the contract *before* getting approval from the bankruptcy court?

On the first issue, the Supreme Court reversed legal precedents in the federal courts by choosing a standard well below that of "imminent failure" of the company. Instead, the Supreme Court argued (in a 9–0 decision) that a bankruptcy court "should permit rejection of a collective bargaining agreement . . . if the debtor can show that the collective bargaining agreement burdens the estate and that after careful scrutiny, the equities balance in favor of rejecting the labor contract" (NLRB v. Bildisco & Bildisco 465 U.S. 526).

The court stated that it had picked a standard somewhere between a simple "business judgment" test and the stricter REA standard of "imminent collapse," but in the opinion written by Chief Justice William Rehnquist, it was clear that the construed goals of bankruptcy law would take precedence over the construed goals of labor law in most cases: "[The court] must focus on the ultimate goal of Chapter 11 when considering those equities. The Bankruptcy Code does not authorize freewheeling consideration of every conceivable equity, but rather only how those equities relate to the success of the reorganization" (465 U.S. 527 [1984]).

The Supreme Court's standard seemed very close to the "business judgment" standard. The company would not have to furnish proof that it would face imminent failure if it did not reject the labor contract. Instead, if a firm wanted to eliminate its labor agreements, it would only have to show that the contract "burden[ed] the estate" and that the balancing of the equities favored rejection. In addition, the language of the decision indicated that the balancing of the equities test should not involve a "freewheeling" consideration of the equities, but only be thought of in relation to how it helps reorganization. It is difficult to envision a case in which rejecting the labor agreement would not in some sense "help" the reorganization, since it would bring lower labor costs. Thus, the Supreme Court decision in Bildisco reversed the trend of preventing labor contract rejection and helped bring the test for rejection into line with the trend of bankruptcy law: helping to keep businesses alive.[6]

On the second issue, whether the NLRB could find Bildisco guilty of an unfair labor practice, the Court decided (in a 5–4 decision) that the company could indeed reject the agreement without first getting the bankruptcy court's approval. Again, the language of the decision reflected bankruptcy law's stress on preserving the business taking precedence over labor law's protection of workers' rights: "[Enforcement of the collective bargaining agreement] would run directly counter to the express provisions of the Bankruptcy Code and to the Code's overall effort to give a debtor-in-possession some flexibility and breathing space" (465 U.S. 532 [1984]).

6. In addition, the decision stated that a company need only show that it had made "reasonable efforts" to negotiate modifications to the labor contract and "that the court need not determine that the parties have bargained to an impasse" (465 U.S. 526).

REACTION TO BILDISCO

Labor leaders could not have reacted more strongly to the Bildisco decision. The day after the decision, Lawrence Gold, special counsel to the AFL-CIO, said, "[Bildisco] will give debtors a practical assurance that collective bargaining agreements may be repudiated with impunity" (Hermann and Neff 1985, 630). Bruce Simon, who had a special interest in the Bildisco case because he was the counsel to the Air Line Pilots Association (representing Continental's pilots), called the decision "the single greatest threat to collective bargaining since the passage of the Wagner Act fifty years ago" (Browning 1984, 60). "[The decision's] the most outrageous goddamned thing I ever heard. We didn't even get out our friends on that one," William Winpisinger, president of the machinists' union, said bluntly, presumably referring to the 9–0 decision on the first issue (36 Daily Labor Report, February 23, 1984, AA-3).

The machinists' and pilots' unions were aware of the impact of this decision on Continental, which was now arguing its case in bankruptcy court. The decision sent a clear message to both sides in the Continental case that the court was likely to hold Continental to a much more lenient standard than the "imminent failure" standard of REA Express. Continental instead would have to show that its labor contracts "burdened the estate" and met the balancing of the equities test. The climate appeared more favorable to Continental and immediately took some of the leverage out of the unions' position. "I think the Bildisco decision gives management another weapon in industries where they need one. . . . I expect that management will begin at least to threaten unions with the possibility of bankruptcy," said Audrey Freeman, a labor economist with the Conference Board (*NYT*, February 2, 1984, D25).[7]

7. Organized labor did not sit idly by after the Bildisco decision. The day the decision was announced, Congressman Peter Rodino (D-N.J.) introduced

THE PROPOSED REORGANIZATION PLAN

By February 1984, Continental had cut its cost per seat-mile by 25 percent. Almost all of this reduction came from the reduction in labor costs from 36 percent of overall costs to 22 percent. The company's cost per seat-mile, a common industry measure, had been cut to about 6 cents from 8.5 cents before the filing (see Securities and Exchange Commission, Continental Airlines 10Q, 10K filings, 1982–84). In addition, the company had built its work force back up to nearly 10,000 from a pre-bankruptcy level of 12,000. It was offering 91 percent of its former service with 20 percent fewer employees, who were being paid much less than in pre-bankruptcy days (table 1).

Continental had achieved the highest load factor in the industry (i.e., its planes were the fullest). This resulted in large part from the simple fact that its fares were now the lowest among all major carriers. Continental had succeeded in reassembling the system it had dismantled. It rehired workers, brought in new employees, and gradually built service back up to nearly the level offered by the "old Continental." By the second quarter of 1984, Continental reported a small profit, as compared to a loss for the same quarter in 1983.

Buoyed by these results, Continental asked the bankruptcy court to free another $600 million in restricted funds to enable the company to purchase thirty new Boeing 737 jets. Continental told the court that it was ready to begin a major expansion plan. This time the banks balked, refusing to free such a large sum of money for fear that it would delay their repayment. Frank Musselman, the lead counsel for Chase

---

a union-supported bill to overturn Bildisco. The eventual outcome (§ 1113 of the Bankruptcy Code) weakens the second part of the Bildisco decision by requiring that the debtor get court approval for the rejection. The test for rejection, however, remains essentially the same (see White 1984, 1171).

Table 1
Selected Indicators of Continental's
Size and Cost Structure

	Pre-bankruptcy (October 1982)	Bankruptcy Filing (October 1983)	During Bankruptcy (December 1983)	Reorganization (September 1985)
Employees	13,500	4,000	5,200	10,000
Cities served	96	50	64	70
Available seat-miles	1,610	589	816	1,400
Cost per seat-mile (in cents)	8.5	...	...	6.3
Passenger load factor (% of seats filled)	57.9%	65.3%	66.8%	...
Labor as % of total operating costs	36%	...	...	22%

SOURCES: SEC documents (Forms 10Q, 10K), company reports, *New York Times*, *Wall Street Journal*, and *Business Week*.

Manhattan, Continental's main creditor, indicated both the helpful role the banks had played in supporting Continental throughout the early stages of the bankruptcy and the reluctance to delay payments to the creditors any further. "The banks have been, up until now, very supportive of Continental's effort to fly itself out of Chapter 11," he said. "It is now time for the company to start paying the creditors back" (*WSJ*, December 28, 1984, 2).

The court sided with the creditors and refused Continental's request that $600 million be freed up for the proposed expansion. Instead, the court permitted Continental to sublease four Boeing 737s from Texas Air. The cost of the sub-leasing was minuscule compared to the original $600 million request.

By January 1985, Continental was ready to offer the first outline of its reorganization plan (the preliminary plan in table 2 below). Continental told the court that it would pay the $1 billion it owed to commercial creditors in full over a period of up to ten years. Several major creditors balked at the ten-year time frame. They wanted the repayment period to be shorter in order to limit their risk in case Continental's reorganization plan should fail. Negotiations began between Continental and the lenders. By September, Continental had agreed to a revised plan (called the final plan in table 2 below). This reorganization plan continued to call for the re-payment in full of the $1 billion in debt, but this time on terms much more favorable to the creditors. The initial pay-ment was higher, the repayment term was much shorter, and the interest rate was higher. On all three counts the com-mercial creditors had improved their position (table 2).

Chase Manhattan's lawyer, Frank Musselman, said of the new plan, "I'm satisfied, it's much better" (*WSJ*, September 5, 1985, 8). By mid-September, most of Continental's com-mercial creditors had agreed to support the plan, and Con-tinental announced that it had arranged for a $50 million line of revolving credit and equipment financing with two groups of banks.

The unions continued to press over $2 billion in claims, including compensation for the wrongful discharge of em-ployees who refused to work at the lower wages offered by the "new Continental" and the lost wages of those who did come back to work, but were paid the lower rate. In a series of decisions announced on September 10 and October 3, Judge T. Glover Roberts dismissed the unions' claims as in-valid, arguing that the employees had not been wrongfully discharged, since he had previously ruled that Continental's abrogation of its labor contracts was legal and justified. On June 30, 1986, Continental's reorganization plan was con-

Table 2
*Comparison of Continental's Preliminary
and Final Reorganization Plans*

	Preliminary Plan		Final Plan	
	Secured Creditors	Unsecured Creditors	Secured Creditors	Unsecured Creditors
Term (years)	10	12–13	8	5
Interest	Prime + 1%	0	Prime + 1%	Prime + 2%
Initial payment	$85 million	. . .	$121 million	. . .

firmed by the bankruptcy court. "From now on, I think we will see much more rational behavior on the part of the unions," Frank Lorenzo told *Fortune* (January 9, 1984, 73).

FOCUSING ON LABOR COSTS

Continental entered the bankruptcy process in a strategic attempt to reduce its labor costs. Lorenzo had said himself in September 1983 that his company's sole problem was labor, and a senior vice president had written that Chapter 11 might provide just "the stick" necessary to get reduced labor costs. Management tried to accomplish its goal of drastic wage concessions through the collective bargaining process. When this proved unsuccessful, Chapter 11 provided a structured setting for Continental to transform a troublesome relationship with its workers into one more beneficial to management. Through its rejection of labor contracts under Chapter 11 bankruptcy, Continental ended up reducing its labor costs as a percentage of overall costs from 36 to 22 percent. "They pulled off a coup," Julius Maldutis, an industry analyst at Salomon Brothers, said flatly (*NYT*, September 24, 1984, 1).

Because of his financial background and previous experience, Lorenzo was seen as representative of a "new breed" of airline executive that understood the changes taking place in the organizational context of the airline industry. Lorenzo stepped in to accelerate those changes. Because of his reputation as a cost-cutter, he was able to attract a large amount of capital from financial markets with his vision for cutting labor costs.

But Continental's management did not make its strategic choices in a vacuum. Rather, the company operated in a constrained environment in which the actions of other organizations had important impacts on Continental's strategic decision-making. Accounting for the organizational environment and the actions of other institutions helps in understanding why management opted for a bankruptcy filing.

Beginning in the late 1970s, drastic changes in the regulatory environment of the airline industry introduced a large dose of competition into what had been a highly regulated oligopoly. The Civil Aeronautics Board reduced the barriers to new, smaller competitors and relaxed regulations on pricing. These legal changes brought competitive pressures to a formerly insulated market. Profits in the airline industry suffered during these early years of deregulation. Airline stock prices slid, and airline management came under increasing pressure to cut costs and restore profitability.

Government action thus altered a business environment that had long provided stability for airlines. The deregulation of the airline industry (at least temporarily) introduced major strains into the relations between Continental and its employees, as well as between Continental and its lenders and suppliers. Many airlines expanded too fast after deregulation, leading to overcapacity in the industry. The combination of the deregulated environment and this overcapacity led to the disintegration of the price discipline airlines had been famous for. Continental faced particularly severe pressure because it had failed to create an automated reservation system as United and American had. These computerized systems, which were in place at 80 percent of the nation's travel agents, provided a competitive edge to United and American and cut into Continental's passenger traffic, adding to the pressure to cut costs.

Because costs in the airline industry do not vary proportionately with levels of passenger traffic, profit levels are extremely sensitive to changes in traffic or fares. When passenger traffic did not meet expectations during the 1970s, fares were slashed. Planes continued to fly at less than capacity, but costs did not drop proportionately, since half-full planes require almost the same fixed costs (fuel, labor, etc.) to fly as full planes. Since labor costs represented a major component of total costs for Continental, this item became the primary focus of management.

But there were other costs that management could have tried to reduce. Fuel, equipment, and capital (interest rates on loans) also represented large costs for Continental. Apparently, these costs were not as amenable to manipulation as labor costs. Reducing the cost of fuel and equipment might have proved more difficult, since it required battling fairly large companies with more power than labor unions to resist. Reducing the cost of money by renegotiating existing loans or obtaining new loans at lower rates seems to have been dismissed out of hand owing to the power of large commercial banks to oppose this. In fact, the banks used their power over Continental management to prevent the airline from borrowing money from its own parent company, Texas Air, even prior to its bankruptcy filing. A Continental official stated that the banks "would not approve" such borrowing.

The vulnerability of organized labor in the 1980s led to the perception that reducing labor costs might be a lot easier than trying to lower fuel or equipment costs or the cost of money. The supply of available labor during Continental's bankruptcy (a time of recession) added to Continental's ability to drastically alter this component of its costs.

Bankruptcy courts had allowed the rejection of labor contracts since at least 1959 (*In re* Klabber Bros. Inc. 173 F.

Supp. 83 [S.D.N.Y. 1959]). With the weakening of the labor movement in the late 1970s and early 1980s, employers increasingly sought to reject bargaining agreements. The changes made in the 1978 bankruptcy law that made it easier for companies to enter Chapter 11 also helped produce more of these cases. James White (1984) in a review of cases involving companies rejecting labor contracts through bankruptcy found over thirty cases, with most occurring in the 1970s and 1980s. In reviewing these cases, it becomes clear that they are clustered in industries with recent deregulation and competition (e.g., airlines and trucking) and in industries with new competition from non-union companies (e.g., meat packing). This indicates that both organizational environment (deregulation) and the relative power of unions (to prevent non-union competition) are important in producing bankruptcies aimed at rejecting labor contracts.

Commercial creditors played a key role in the case. While Frank Lorenzo played the visible lead in cutting costs in a deregulated environment, he was backed by large institutional lenders. Lorenzo got very strong support from lenders both in his early career and throughout the Chapter 11 process. Chase Manhattan funded many of his efforts early in his career. In his attempt to take over Continental, Lorenzo was again supported by Chase Manhattan, which made the crucial decision to back his takeover attempt rather than the employees' proposal to buy the company. This decision was apparently based on the assumption that the employees would insist on higher wages, which would destroy the company. As we have seen, the lenders preferred the cost-cutting strategy proposed by management to the ESOP proposed by employees. During the bankruptcy itself, commercial creditors were important parties to Continental's strategic decision-making.

Continental's ability to declare bankruptcy while still holding substantial liquid assets enabled the company to cut fares and retain its credibility with the public immediately upon filing for Chapter 11. Consumers buying Continental tickets demonstrated that they had begun to accept the notion of bankruptcy as a strategy, suggesting that they too understood that the filing did not mean that the company was broke.

Although Continental's competitors reacted by matching some of Continental's reduced fares, they could only do this to a limited degree, since their labor costs were much higher than those of the "new Continental." Continental's competitors (with costs of 8 cents per seat-mile versus Continental's 6 cents) chose to match Continental's fares only when they feared losing market share to Continental.

Through the bankruptcy filing, Continental managed to achieve a cost structure far superior to those of other major airlines. The company reduced labor costs from 36 percent of its total operating budget to 22 percent. Based on these labor savings, Continental began earning a profit again in 1984. To a large degree, Continental became the "fare-setter" for the rest of the industry, increasing the pressure on other airlines to reduce costs.[8] In 1987, after having to back off on a plan to increase restrictions on its reduced rate fares, Robert Crandall of American Airlines said (referring to Continental), "Whoever has the lowest costs can set the prices" (*Business Week*, March 16, 1987).

In this case, Continental's claim to bankruptcy was constructed in four ways: (1) the definition of the "bankrupt unit"; (2) the definition of assets belonging to that unit and, therefore, subject to bankruptcy claims; (3) management action to legitimate the claim to "bankrupt" status; and (4) action to legitimate bankruptcy as a dignified status in the public mind.

Continental was able to gain court approval of its definition of what constituted the "bankrupt unit." The unions and creditors both tried to get Texas Air included in the bankruptcy process, so that they could make claims on those as-

8. Later, Frank Lorenzo's Eastern Air Lines would also declare bankruptcy in an effort to reduce labor costs.

sets as well as on the assets of Continental. By declaring that Continental was a separate company from Texas Air, Continental was able to legitimate its claim to bankruptcy, raising questions about what really constitutes "a company." Obviously this was more than a semantic argument. If Texas Air had been included as part of the debtor in the case, the unions might have succeeded in their argument that the filing was in "bad faith" and that the firm was not really bankrupt. Which assets and debts get counted are obviously crucial to the definition of "bankrupt."[9]

After the court accepted Continental's definition of what constituted the "bankrupt unit," the definition of assets belonging to the bankrupt unit continued to produce competing interpretations. The unions charged that Continental had moved assets either to the parent company or to other nonunion subsidiaries before the filing, thereby substantiating the claim to bankruptcy and leaving fewer assets available to creditors and workers.

Continental management took actions that precipitated the strike of all of Continental's unionized employees. Once the strikes occurred, the firm could easily substantiate its claim to "equity insolvency"—that future debts would overwhelm future assets.

At the time of the filing, Continental did not face a cash-flow crisis. It retained $58 million in cash and probably could have continued without bankruptcy. It might have continued to lose money and not have retained the cash "cushion" that eventually proved decisive in its first month under Chapter 11. Continental had learned from the Braniff bankruptcy how important it was to declare Chapter 11 early.

Continental was also successful in gaining control of cash collateral at crucial points during the case. In two instances

9. Not long after the approval of Continental's reorganization plan, Texas Air acquired all of the outstanding shares of Continental. Once labor costs were reduced, Texas Air was willing to make Continental a wholly owned subsidiary.

during the first few weeks of the case, Continental was able to gain a total of $40 million in formerly "restricted assets" (assets reserved to cover pre-bankruptcy debts). Continental gained court approval to substitute new receivables, less liquid, as collateral. With this $40 million, Continental was able to reduce its fares, rehire striking pilots, hire new employees, and convince its creditors that its reorganization had a good chance of working. Thus, the favorable interpretation of such seemingly technical terms as *assets, collateral,* and *restricted assets* was crucial to Continental's ability to weather the strike and the bankruptcy filing.

This case also illustrates the importance of the legal and social changes outlined in chapter 1. The old Bankruptcy Act of 1898 required a showing of insolvency before a company could file for reorganization. However, that provision was removed from the 1978 Act when Congress tried to broaden the conditions under which a firm can enter Chapter 11. Continental might not have been able to meet the 1898 insolvency tests, particularly if the unions had been successful in their arguments regarding the movement of assets among subsidiaries. But, as we have seen, bankruptcy law now permits companies to get into the Chapter 11 process without meeting a traditional insolvency test. A company may enter Chapter 11 based on an "equity insolvency" test by arguing that it will not be able to meet *future* debts owing to a long-term labor contract. Once future debts and assets are considered as opposed to actual or current debts and assets, the possibility of widely varying interpretations of these future assets and debts becomes a major issue facing the court. The fact that Continental's employees were out on strike helped the company's claim to equity insolvency, since it made it fairly easy to demonstrate that the firm's assets would soon be overwhelmed by its liabilities.

In this case, the broadened definition of *bankrupt* led to a clash with labor law's protection of legally negotiated collective bargaining agreements. Varying legal definitions of when rejection of a contract is necessary for a company to survive illustrate the power of the court to define a "business crisis." In recent years, courts have set a variety of legal standards that companies had to meet in order to reject a labor contract. Each of these tests was vague and subject to interpretation, but the trend was clear. Throughout the 1970s, the courts were moving in the direction of making it more difficult for firms to reject contracts by strengthening the test for rejection. For example, the standard of REA Express required the company to show that if it did not violate its labor agreement, it would face "imminent collapse." This, however, flew in the face of the trend occurring in the bankruptcy arena that stressed the preservation of the company, even if that meant rejecting labor agreements.

In Bildisco, the Supreme Court decided that in the clash between labor and bankruptcy law, bankruptcy law's stress on preserving the company was more important. The Court declared that the debtor did not have to provide proof that it would collapse without the rejection of the contract. Instead, the debtor merely had to show that the contract "burdened the estate" and that the "equities balanced" in favor of the rejection. Several legal commentators have argued that they constitute little more than the simple "business judgment" test (Bordewieck and Countryman 1983; White 1984, 1198).

Continental's position was greatly enhanced by this new legal test, which was declared during Continental's time under Chapter 11 protection. Although all of the standards are subject to wide interpretation (e.g., interpretations of "imminent collapse," "burdening of the estate," and "balancing the equities" are all problematic), Continental would certainly have had an easier time meeting the Bildisco standard than the REA Express standard. The Bildisco decision strengthened Continental management's position because it made clear that the Supreme Court was likely to uphold its bankruptcy filing and its rejection of collective bargaining agreements. The Court had elevated bankruptcy law over labor law. The trend toward expanding the bankruptcy arena and preserving the company at all costs had been confirmed and extended a step further by the Supreme Court.

CONCLUSION

Unlike the Manville case, in which large commercial creditors actively constrained the company's choices and precipitated the crisis, Continental management seemed to be choosing Chapter 11 as strategy in anticipation of lender action. Lorenzo had a wealth of experience as a cost-cutter in the airline industry, and Continental's strategic bankruptcy was a logical extension of this effort. The Continental case thus represents another step in the use of bankruptcy to accomplish limited organizational objectives. Although there is no direct evidence, I think this case suggests that institutional learning occurred as top managers monitored the strategic bankruptcies of other firms, increasing their willingness to try the strategy themselves. Although rejection of labor contracts through bankruptcy had been around since at least 1959, these cases tended to occur in smaller firms with less powerful unions. The emergence of strategic bankruptcy, changes in bankruptcy law, and the weakening of union power made contract rejection more likely now even by the largest U.S. firms with unionized employees.

It is hard to argue that bankruptcy acted as a market mechanism or a neutral debt-collection device in this case as legal doctrinal and economic theories posit. The Chapter 11 process is supposed to weed out inefficient firms and allow efficient firms to stay in business. Continental's management had made a number of missteps, including the failure to build a reservation system. But despite managerial blunders and a number of competitive disadvantages, the firm was able to use the bankruptcy process to negate its labor contracts and stay in business. This case illustrates the political and strategic nature of bankruptcy. The airline was able to abrogate legally negotiated contracts to achieve the best labor costs in the industry through a planned bankruptcy.

The political nature of bankruptcy is also revealed in the clash between labor law and bankruptcy law. Continental's abrogation of its labor contracts was a clear violation of labor law and collective bargaining procedure. Bankruptcy law, however, permits the rejection of executory contracts (those not yet performed). Much more is at stake when these contracts are rejected than monetary issues. Rejection of a union contract can include rejection of seniority rules, grievance procedures, work rules, and issues won by the union through bargaining. In the case of Continental, bankruptcy law—which tends to protect capital—thus triumphed over labor law, which is more likely to protect workers' rights. It is hard to see the fairness of the bankruptcy process here. It is clear that organized labor had less clout than commercial creditors and management.

The social construction of bankruptcy in this case involved not only interpretations of law but also the very definition of what constitutes a company. As in the Manville case, the Continental bankruptcy demonstrates that balance-sheet figures cannot be taken at face value. Instead, we must ask: What assets and liabilities get included as part of that corporate unit deemed bankrupt? This case shows that the shifting of assets among corporate entities can ensure access to the Chapter 11 process.[10]

10. After the Continental bankruptcy, Congress came under tremendous pressure from organized labor to rewrite the bankruptcy law to prevent similar cases. Congress delineated a nine-point test for the rejection of collective bargaining agreements in the Bankruptcy Amendment and Federal Judgeship Act of 1984 (Pub. L. No. 98-353 [1984]). In essence, the test codifies the standard of rejection in the Bildisco case while limiting a company's ability to reject a labor contract without attempting to negotiate with the union. Many of the points in the test relate to informing the union of proposed modifications to the contract. However, the language of the nine-point test is open for interpretation. For example, it requires that the debtor company treat all parties fairly and that the balance of equities favor rejection of the contract. In the bankruptcies that have occurred since Continental and involve rejection of union contracts, the courts have generally looked at whether rejection was necessary to permit a successful reorganization (Vian 1986, 252–66). As I have argued throughout this book, the answer to this question is in the eye of the beholder.

5

Texaco:
Using Bankruptcy to
Frustrate a Business Rival

[The Texaco case raises questions about] the propriety
of declaring bankruptcy to frustrate a business rival.
. . . When a solvent company files for bankruptcy
many laymen are likely to suspect that the company
is merely dodging its obligations.
—American Bar Association Journal,
August 1, 1987

YOU CAN TRUST YOUR CAR
TO THE MAN WHO WEARS THE STAR

Joseph Cullinan found black gold in "them thar' hills" when
he discovered oil on Spindletop in Beaumont, Texas, in 1901.
The next year, Cullinan, a former employee of Standard Oil,
formed the Texas Company to take advantage of his good
fortune. By 1928, the Texas Company was operating in all 48
states and was touted as a corporate success story that embodied the "American Dream."[1]

In 1936 the company ventured overseas for the first time,
teaming with Standard Oil of California to market oil from
the Middle East. The Texas Company also purchased an in-

1. This section draws in part on historical sketches provided by Petzinger
1987 and *Time*, April 20, 1987.

126

terest in California Arabian Standard Oil, which in turn held a major concession in Saudi Arabia. That venture later became Aramco, a major consortium of Saudi and American oil producers.

The oil firm's express hit its first speed bump in 1940, when its chairman was forced to resign after a company representative in Germany was found to be a Nazi collaborator. The employee had illegally obtained a report on the U.S. aircraft industry prepared by the Texas Company's staff of economists.

This bout of bad publicity ended fairly quickly, and the Texas Company enjoyed further success as the nation's #1 oil company through the 1950s and 1960s, when it came to be known as Texaco. Texaco hit its peak in the 1950s, when "millions of Americans watched the *Texaco Star Theatre* television show, featuring Milton Berle, and a decade later any child could sing the jingle, 'You can trust your car to the man who wears the star'" (*Time*, April 20, 1987, 52).

But the world of oil was changing. Middle Eastern countries became major players on the world scene in the 1970s, when the acronym OPEC (Organization of Petroleum Exporting Countries) began to dominate the national news. Long gas lines and checking the last digit of your license plate to determine if you were "odd" or "even" became a part of daily life in the United States. Texaco, like other U.S.–based oil companies, could no longer count on world dominance.

Texaco's troubles seemed even greater than those of some of the other U.S. oil giants. Throughout the 1970s and 1980s, Texaco's oil reserves dwindled, and many of its retail gasoline stations folded. Texaco began to gain a reputation in the industry as a company that had trouble finding new oil. Between 1972 and 1980, Texaco's oil reserves fell more rapidly than those of any other major oil company (*Business Week*, December 9, 1985, 36). In the years from 1979 to 1984, Texaco's reserves fell by one-fifth (*Economist*, January 14, 1984, 16). To find each barrel of oil and gas, Texaco spent close to

$15, as compared to an industry average of about $10 per barrel. By 1977, Texaco had lost its #1 ranking among U.S. oil companies, falling into third place behind Exxon and Mobil.

Of course, with assets in excess of $37 billion, annual revenues of about $46 billion, and a ranking as the nation's seventh largest corporation, Texaco remained a powerful corporate player. But the company had fallen out of favor with Wall Street oil analysts. Texaco was frequently portrayed as a sleepy, sluggish corporate giant, and Wall Street pressured the company to shed some of its unprofitable assets.

Texaco responded in the early 1980s by closing 18,000 gas stations and beginning a $9 billion effort to locate new oil and gas. However, a partnership between Texaco and Standard Oil spent $1.7 billion searching for new oil and came up with virtually nothing. Once again Wall Street analysts chided Texaco's failure to find new oil. At some point during 1983, Texaco made the decision to try to acquire what it could not locate itself, and in 1984 it announced the acquisition of the Getty Oil Company. Texaco did not know it at the time, but this acquisition would lead to a major court battle with Pennzoil, a smaller oil company, whose corporate predecessor had been founded by Hugh Liedtke and George Bush in 1953. The Getty deal would eventually lead to the largest bankruptcy filing in the history of the United States.

THE GETTY ACQUISITION

In late 1983, Gordon Getty, the son of the late J. Paul Getty and the sole trustee of the Sarah Getty trust (which controlled 40 percent of Getty stock), attempted to take full control of Getty Oil (*Economist*, January 14, 1984, 67–68). He hired the investment banking partnership Goldman Sachs to do a "valuation analysis" of the company. Through his actions, Gordon Getty inadvertently set off a takeover battle for the company by alerting many in the oil industry that Getty Oil was "in play" (Petzinger 1987, 101). The *Wall Street Journal* and other business sources began carrying continual rumors of a Getty takeover.

Although Getty ranked only fourteenth among oil companies in terms of annual sales, it held 1.5 billion barrels of oil in U.S. soil, making it an attractive company for an oil giant with dwindling reserves (Petzinger 1987, 70). On December 28, 1983, Pennzoil, the nation's twentieth largest oil company, made a public tender offer for 20 percent of Getty stock for $100 per share. During the next week, Pennzoil privately came to a separate agreement with Getty's board of directors to acquire 42 percent of Getty stock (including 12 percent owned by the J. Paul Getty Museum) for $112.50 per share.

On January 3, 1984, the Pennzoil Company's board of directors endorsed a memorandum of understanding to acquire 42 percent of Getty Oil, including one billion barrels of crude oil reserves, for $112.50 per share, or $5.3 billion. The Pennzoil deal would have turned Getty into a private company in partnership with Gordon Getty. The following day, January 4, both Pennzoil and Getty issued press releases detailing the proposed merger. The releases stated that the parties had reached an "agreement in principle" and that the transaction was subject to the execution of a definitive agreement.

That same day, Texaco learned that formal papers had not yet been signed by the two oil companies and began its own plan to acquire Getty. On January 5, the Texaco board agreed to pursue a $10.3 billion offer for all of the outstanding shares of Getty at $125 per share.

On January 6, Getty's board voted to accept the new, higher offer from Texaco. The next day, Getty issued a second press release, this time announcing the sale of the company to Texaco. Pennzoil immediately notified Getty of its objections to the Texaco takeover, demanding that Getty abide by the original Pennzoil-Getty agreement. But Getty now had a better deal with Texaco.

Notwithstanding the possible legal tangle, the acquisition was hailed by most in the business community as a wise move by Texaco. The acquisition of Getty would immediately stop the depletion of Texaco's reserves, providing time for its new $9 billion exploration effort to pay off. The addition of Getty would double Texaco's oil reserves from 1.9 billion barrels to 3.9 billion barrels, at a cost to Texaco of only $5 per barrel, well below the $12 per barrel it was spending to find the oil itself. The *Economist* (January 14, 1984, 16) reported that "Texaco is sensibly buying itself an oil company." But Texaco ended up "buying" a lot more than it had expected.

TEXACO VERSUS PENNZOIL

Texaco's acquisition of Getty began a legal battle that was to dominate the pages of the business press for months. On February 8, 1984, Pennzoil filed several lawsuits in the Houston courts charging Getty with breach of contract and Texaco with illegally inducing Getty to break its contract with Pennzoil. In court papers, Pennzoil argued that it had a handshake, a directors' vote, and a press release proving that it had a deal with Getty. Texaco argued that with no written contract, there was no deal.

The case essentially revolved around two very basic legal issues: (1) Was there an enforceable contract? (2) If so, what were the damages to Pennzoil for the breach of this contract? (see Texaco Inc. v. Pennzoil Co., 784 F.2d 1133, 1138 [2d Cir. 1986]).

When Is a Deal a Deal?

The vast majority of the testimony in the four and a half months of the Texaco-Pennzoil case centered on what seemed like a narrow, technical legal question, but was actually a social question centering on how we define "routine business practice." When are the parties bound to a deal? Pennzoil argued that the moment the Getty board of directors accepted the memorandum of understanding, they had agreed to be bound by the terms of the deal. Pennzoil presented a press release issued jointly by Pennzoil and Getty as evidence that they indeed had a "done deal." Texaco, on the other hand, argued that a deal is not a deal until the final terms are put on paper and the parties sign a formal document. Texaco argued that the press release explicitly stated that the agreement in principle was subject to the execution of a definitive merger agreement.

The area of law covering such a dispute is called "The Law of Agreements in Principle with a Formal Contract Contemplated" (see American Law Institute 1981, 78–79). The key question was simply, When are the parties legally bound to the deal? This was important, since once the parties are considered bound by the agreement, any deviation from, or refusal to follow, its terms could result in a breach of contract.

For several months, lawyers for both sides presented their arguments on the issue to a Houston courtroom. The jury, however, deliberated for only eleven hours and found in favor of Pennzoil on the first issue; that is, an enforceable contract did exist between Pennzoil and Getty, and Texaco had interfered with that contract by inducing Getty to break the agreement.

Apparently, the jury had reasoned that a "handshake and an agreement in principle" were enough to constitute a deal among major players in the Texas oil patch. Pennzoil's lawyers cleverly portrayed Texaco as an "East Coast company" (headquartered in White Plains, N.Y.) dominated by "Wall Street types" from New York, while Pennzoil was merely a hometown company trying to do business the old-fashioned way: with a handshake (Petzinger 1987; *NYT*, December 12, 1985, D1).[2]

---

2. It is ironic that Texaco (with its origins as the Texas Company) ended up portrayed as an East Coast firm, while Pennzoil (with its origins as Pennsylvania Oil) ended up as the "good ol' boy" Texas company. This reversal in the public mind occurred because each company's headquarters had migrated across the country.

Much of the testimony centered on the "etiquette" followed by "Texas Oil Men" (*sic*) when they conduct business. Pennzoil's colorful CEO, Hugh Liedtke, accused Texaco of not following those rules, telling the court that "dealing with Texaco was like trying to frisk a wet seal" (*Economist*, December 14, 1985, 86). Pennzoil's lead trial attorney, Joe Jamail, played heavily on the idea that a person's word is as important as any written document, telling the court, "This is a case of promises and what those promises meant to Pennzoil, and what they ultimately meant to Texaco" (Petzinger 1987, 22). One business writer summed up the flavor of the trial, calling it a matchup between "a haughty New York Goliath vs. a feisty hometown David" (*Business Week*, December 9, 1985, 36).

Despite the popular appeal and dramatic flair of Pennzoil's trial strategy, the decision by the Houston jury shook many in the legal and financial world. "Prior to the Pennzoil decision, mergers and acquisitions specialists believed that parties became bound only after the signing of a formal agreement" (Goffinet 1987, 1369). Investment bankers worried that this decision would dampen the bidding process when a company became a takeover target. "Until Pennzoil, specialists in the securities field observed that such a [press] release provides notice to any other corporation wishing to enter the bidding war that the target is for sale and that parties are not yet contractually bound" (ibid. 1378). The Pennzoil decision made "the rules of contract law regarding the formal contract contemplated . . . imprecise and uncertain" (ibid. 1396).

How Much Damage Was Done?

Many legal and financial analysts were surprised by the jury's finding on the first issue. They expressed further shock when the jury awarded Pennzoil $7.53 billion in compensatory damages and $3 billion in punitive damages. The total of $10.53 billion was by far the largest court award in history. In fact, according to one Texaco lawyer, the award was forty times bigger than the largest private civil judgment ever to withstand appeal in any prior case of any kind (Bainbridge 1987, 111).

Early on in the case, Texaco's lawyers had made the tactical decision *not* to present any evidence at all to the jury on the issue of damages. They reasoned that by shifting gears from arguing that there was absolutely no contract to presenting evidence on what the damages should be *if* there were a contract would weaken their original argument over the very existence of an enforceable contract.

In hindsight, the decision proved to be a major blunder. The jury was left with only Pennzoil's evidence regarding damages. On this issue, Pennzoil argued that the formula for assessing the damage to the company would be to find the difference between what it would cost Pennzoil to acquire Getty's reserves and what it would have cost Pennzoil to go out and find the one billion barrels of oil through its own exploration efforts.

In many ways, this seemed like a strange way to calculate the damages. For one thing, if Pennzoil had been horribly inefficient at finding oil throughout its corporate history, it would be rewarded for this inefficiency by receiving larger damages than if it had been incredibly good at oil exploration. For example, using the same logic, if a non-oil company had tried to take over Getty and lost out to Texaco as Pennzoil did, it could argue that it would cost it "zillions" of dollars to find the oil, since it knew absolutely nothing about oil exploration. The difference between "zillions" and the acquisition price for Getty would result in the non-oil company being granted a huge award for damages.

Moreover, estimating how much it would cost Pennzoil to find the oil was a very tricky process. Despite the presence of geological engineers and other scientific professionals, oil exploration is often a crapshoot. In fact, Texaco and Standard Oil had recently demonstrated the "hit or miss" nature of oil exploration by spending $1.7 billion on a project that came up virtually empty. Pennzoil presented the jury with numbers on what it would have cost it to find the oil itself. Texaco certainly would have presented a much different set of numbers if it had decided to argue along these grounds.

There were alternate ways to calculate damages. One way would have been to calculate the difference between what Pennzoil would have paid for Getty and what it would now have to pay to buy the same amount of oil in the open market or through another acquisition. This would have yielded a much smaller damage award, essentially the amount Pennzoil lost as a result of missing the opportunity to acquire Getty and having instead to acquire the oil somewhere else. Another possible formula (which in fact would be employed by an appellate judge later in the case) calculates the damages as the difference between what Pennzoil would have paid for Getty ($112.50 per share) and what Texaco eventually paid ($125 per share). This formula yields a damage award of $800 million, smaller than the Houston award by more than a factor of ten.

In the weeks following the jury verdict, numerous commentators attacked the damage award as "absurd," including a *Washington Post* editorialist (November 21, 1985, A26), the *Oil Daily* trade newspaper (November 21, 1985, 1), and a federal appeals judge (Texaco Inc. v. Pennzoil Co., 784 F.2d 1133 [2d Cir. 1986]). Professor Robert Mnookin of Stanford Law School bluntly stated: "Most impartial observers would agree that the jury's damage award was absurdly high and bore no real relation to Pennzoil's actual damages" (*NYT*, December 19, 1987, D1).

THE FINANCIAL COMMUNITY REACTS

The damage award introduced a huge strain into Texaco's relationship with other important players in the firm's network. Texaco's financial status, of course, suffered a serious blow owing to the $10.53 billion judgment. The company did, however, have over $35 billion in assets, a healthy cash flow, annual revenues in excess of $32 billion, and equity of over $13 billion. At one point, Texaco argued in court documents that its assets were more than adequate to pay Pennzoil the $10.53 billion if it lost its appeals (*NYT*, April 14, 1987, D1).

Although Texaco had lost the first round of its legal battle with Pennzoil, it still had many cards left to play in the appeals process. The most important of these included Texaco's charge that Pennzoil had violated Securities and Exchange Commission rules in its takeover attempt. Recall that Pennzoil first made a public tender offer for 20 percent of the outstanding Getty shares at $100 per share on December 28, 1983. The following week, Pennzoil arrived at a separate, privately negotiated agreement with Getty's board to acquire 42 percent of the company at $112.50. Texaco charged that this violated SEC rules against what is called "going outside the tender offer"—that is, negotiating a private agreement while a public tender offer is still in effect (see Securities and Exchange Commission Rule 10b-13). Texaco planned to argue on appeal that even if Pennzoil did indeed have an agreement with Getty, the SEC violation voided the contract.

Texaco planned to appeal the compensatory and punitive damage awards. Many business and legal experts felt that the damages bore little relation to the actual damages suffered by Pennzoil, though what Texaco thought the true damages were remained unclear. In addition, Texaco planned to challenge Judge Solomon Casseb's instructions to the Houston jury, which it felt had improperly biased the jury toward finding that an enforceable contract existed. The judge had told the jury that an "agreement in principle expressly subject to a definitive agreement" constitutes an enforceable contract (Funkhouser et al. 1986, 1367). In all, Texaco would later assert 130 errors in its formal appeal (*Oil Daily*, June 17, 1987, 1). Throughout this period, Texaco and Pennzoil held sporadic talks aimed at fashioning a settlement to their dispute. Rumors swirled that Pennzoil might settle for something in the neighborhood of $6 billion, but Texaco was only offering $1 billion.

Regardless of Texaco's optimism regarding the chances of its appeal, the oil giant's lenders quickly acted, helping to precipitate a crisis for Texaco. The lenders began to apply pressure to force Texaco and Pennzoil to settle the case (*NYT*, December 12, 1985, D1). One day after the Houston judgment, Texaco had great difficulty trying to sell commercial paper on the market (ibid.). The rating on the company's long-term debt was immediately lowered from A-1 to Ba-1 by Moody's, making the damaging jump from "investment grade" to "speculative grade" in Moody's rating scheme (*Economist*, December 14, 1985, 86). The rating on Texaco's outstanding commercial paper was lowered from "prime" to "not prime." All of these actions immediately made it difficult for Texaco to borrow funds at competitive rates. Unsecured borrowing was simply not available from any bank, and Texaco even found secured loans difficult to obtain (Texaco v. Pennzoil, 784 F.2d 1139).

In addition, Texaco's bankers instituted new restrictions on the movement of money within Texaco's own accounts and new minimum balance requirements for its existing accounts (*Time*, April 20, 1987, 50). An analyst for the investment firm First Boston observed that the trial court judgment and the financial community's reaction to it were going to paralyze Texaco "unless they find a way around it" (*NYT*, December 12, 1985, D1).

Although these actions seemed to be solely a result of the Houston verdict, several banking officials interviewed by the *New York Times* (December 12, 1985, D1) seemed to indicate that there was something more at work:

> Bankers said they were still bitter about the way Texaco had treated them in the past. For example, in the past Texaco has gone directly to banks around the country arranging its own revolving credit instead of taking the usual route of asking

one or two major banks to arrange a syndicate. "If it were Exxon or Mobil, all the big banks would rally around it," said one New York banker.

But this was not just a matter of wounded pride or a chance at revenge. By refusing to use syndicate financing in the past, Texaco had been able to negotiate better terms and avoid restrictive covenants that might have been imposed by a coordinated banking syndicate. Texaco had been able to do this in the past owing to its financial strength. Now that the court award put the company on the ropes, the banks saw their chance to make Texaco comply with their rules in the future.

An official at a credit-rating firm asked, "The question now is will the banks step forward with lending facilities like they did for the Getty acquisition, or will they cite 'material adverse developments' as a reason for backing out of loan agreements?" (*NYT*, December 12, 1985, D1). The financial community watched closely as the appeals process began.

THE APPEALS PROCESS

As soon as Judge Casseb officially entered the jury's judgment into court records, Texaco would be forced to pay the $10.53 billion award. Texas law contains what is called a mandatory "supersedeas" bond requirement demanding that any party subject to a judgment post a bond equal to the judgment, plus interest and costs, in order to appeal (Tex. Rev. Civ. Stat. ¶ 364). If Texaco appealed the case, it would be required to post a bond equal to the judgment, interest, and costs, then totaling approximately $11 billion.

Texaco immediately filed a federal appeal in the southern district of New York challenging the bond requirement. Texaco argued that the Texas bond requirement would deprive the company of its due process rights under the Fourteenth Amendment: "No state shall . . . deprive any person of life, liberty or property, without due process of law." Texaco alleged that the bond was so large that it was financially "impracticable" to post (Carlson 1987, 29) and would thereby deprive the company of its constitutional right to appeal.

As several legal scholars (Carlson 1987; Stein 1986) have pointed out, however, although the due process clause had been construed to mandate that "all citizens shall enjoy free and open access to the courts of the United States to obtain redress from injury" (Armstrong v. Manzo, 380 U.S. 545, 550–52 [1965]), the Supreme Court had *not* required that individual states provide open access to their *appellate* courts in civil or criminal cases (McKane v. Durston, 153 U.S. 684 [1894]; Griffin v. Illinois, 351 U.S. 958 [1956]; Lindsey v. Normet, 405 U.S. 56 [1971]; Ortwein v. Schwab, 410 U.S. 656 [1973]; Jones v. Barnes, 463 U.S. 745, 751 [1983]). In these cases, the Court ruled that the Fourteenth Amendment guarantees that all citizens have one chance at the court system but does not guarantee the right to an appeal.

Ironically, most of the case law in this area revolves around the rights of indigents who cannot afford an appeal. In a strange twist, Texaco, the nation's seventh largest industrial company, was arguing that it was now like an indigent barred from a fair hearing because of lack of money.

It is important to note, however, that Texaco did not argue that it was *unable* to post the bond, only that it was "financially impracticable" to post it. Texaco probably wanted to reassure its suppliers and customers that it would not be broke if it were forced to pay the bond. Texaco had assets of approximately $37 billion, but in order to post an $11 billion bond, it would have had to begin selling valuable assets, close down some operations, and lay off employees. Texaco *could* have posted the bond, but only after liquidating assets.

Despite the legal precedents, the federal district court in New York ruled in favor of Texaco, providing it with an injunction against the imposition of the supersedeas bond requirement, based on Texaco's right to an appeal. A legal scholar called the decision "rather remarkable" in light of previous case law and a clear "break with the McKane doctrine" holding that the right to appeal was not guaranteed under the Fourteenth Amendment (Stein 1986, 476). The court seemed to be willing to make an exception for Texaco that it had not made for indigent individuals. As in the Continental case, crucial breaks with past legal precedents bring other aspects of the law (in Continental, labor law, and in this case, the Fourteenth Amendment right to due process) into line with bankruptcy law's inherent stress on keeping companies intact. Thus, the federal district court as well as the bankruptcy court was enforcing the spirit of the new bankruptcy act.

The appeals court approved of the "wise use of discretion" by the district court, reasoning that "[if] a defendant has to liquidate all or a substantial part of his business in order to exercise the right of appeal, then the appeal may surely be of doubtful value" (TWA v. Hughes, 515, F.2d 173 [2d Cir. 1973]). It seemed clear that the court was interested in protecting Texaco in the sense of keeping it together and avoiding any breakup of assets. The Texas court and the federal court received many *amicus curiae* ("friend of the court") briefs suggesting that the earlier bond verdict be reduced or overturned "because of the adverse economic impact it would have . . . on certain states and industries, and on Texaco's many shareholders" (see Goffinet 1987; Texaco v. Pennzoil, 729 S.W. 2d 866 [Tex. Ct. App. 1987, at 865]). The court itself seemed to take these factors into consideration, stating that requiring Texaco to post the bond might "force the appellant into bankruptcy or liquidation," a clear example of enforcing the spirit of the bankruptcy law's increasing stress on keeping firms intact. Texaco claimed, and the court concurred, that the "enforcement of [the bond], along with the simultaneous attachment of property, would render Texaco unable to finance its operations or obtain the credit necessary for its continued existence" (Smith 1987, 632; Texaco v. Pennzoil, 784 F.2d 1152).

But why should the court be so averse to liquidation? The bankruptcy process is supposed to liquidate inefficient firms, and perhaps Texaco would be more efficient if broken up into smaller regional companies. After all, many Wall Street analysts were at the same time arguing that leveraged buy-outs increased the value of a business because they often forced management to sell off pieces of a huge firm, forming smaller, more productive companies. The case for this, of course, had not been proven, but it illustrates that there was a competing economic logic against the position that a huge company is more valuable if kept together. In the Texaco case, there was no serious analysis of this competing position, since Texaco management remained in control of the company and the courts wished to keep the company intact.

In an effort to avoid forcing the oil giant into bankruptcy, the court began to distinguish between the "financial inability" and the "financial impracticability" of posting the bond. Texaco argued that "Texas procedure required it to post a supersedeas bond ... which was financially impracticable" (Texaco v. Pennzoil, 626 F.Supp. 250 [S.D.N.Y.]). No one could argue that Texaco did not have the $11 billion to cover the bond: "The court determined that Texaco's assets were substantially in excess of the approximately $11 billion judgment ... but that the commercial bonding industry could not facilitate Texaco obtaining a bond in this amount. Further, the court found that absent a stay of the Texas trial court judgment, Texaco would probably be forced into bankruptcy or liquidation" (Carlson 1987, 37).

The court drew another crucial linguistic distinction: "The appellant may be financially solvent but not substantially liquid," indicating that it wished to avoid any sale of assets. It seems that the court was driven by the desire to avoid a major breakup of Texaco before the company had a chance to appeal the case. However, it is hard to imagine the court making the same effort for an individual or for a smaller company: "Mr. Smith, you do not need to post the $1,000 bond in order to appeal, because we know that you would be forced to sell your car in order to come up with money, and that certainly would be 'financially impracticable.'

Therefore, since you are solvent, but not liquid, you need not sell your car to post bond."

In fact in Ortwein v. Schwab (410 U.S. 656, 660 [1973]), the court upheld a $25 filing fee for civil appeals as applied to indigents as violating neither the due process nor the equal protection clauses of the Constitution. Neither the "financial impracticability" nor the "financial impossibility" of paying a filing fee for an indigent were viewed as grounds for overturning the law. The judge in the Texaco case seemed to realize the sharp break with past legal precedent, emphasizing that his decision reflected "the extraordinary facts of the case, which are unlikely ever again to recur" (Texaco v. Pennzoil, 784, F.2d 1157; Stein 1986, 463).

Judge Charles Brieant, however, went even further than simply providing a temporary injunction against the bond requirement. On January 10, 1986, he calculated his own version of the damages and ruled that Texaco need only post a $1 billion bond to pursue its appeals. Recall that the original jury sided with Pennzoil's argument that the damages would be calculated by the difference between what it cost Pennzoil to acquire Getty's oil and what it would have cost to find the oil on its own. Pennzoil argued that this formula resulted in damages of $7.53 billion. The jury tacked on $3 billion in punitive damages, for a total award of $10.53 billion.

Judge Brieant, however, ruled that this procedure was "absurd," and that the correct calculation of damages was the difference between what Pennzoil would have paid for Getty ($112.50 per share) and what Texaco eventually paid ($125 per share). This formula yielded damages of only $800 million. Brieant tacked on interest and court costs for total damages of $1 billion, a figure ten times smaller than the original damage award. Brieant argued that no punitive damages could have been awarded under New York law, and that an appeals court would find that New York law rather than Texas law should apply in the case (Texaco v. Pennzoil, 784 F.2d 1133 [2d Cir. 1986]).

On appeal, the Second Circuit court held that Brieant had properly exercised jurisdiction over Texaco's due process and equal protection claims and had properly granted an injunction against the assertion of the $11 billion award. However, with regard to the other aspect of Brieant's decision, the circuit court criticized Brieant for "impermissible" appellate review of issues already adjudicated by the Texas court, including the recalculation of damages (Texaco v. Pennzoil, *aff'd in part, rev'd in part*, 784 F.2d 1133 [2d Cir. 1986]). Some legal theorists argued that the Second Circuit court was also reluctant to see the breakup of Texaco before it was given the chance to appeal: "The potential devastation of one of the nation's largest corporations inevitably weighed heavily on the three members of the [Second Circuit court] panel" (Funkhouser et al. 1986, 822).

At this stage, Texaco was left with a partial and temporary victory. It had achieved a temporary injunction against the collection of damages, but it had no definitive decision on a reduction in damages. This meant that Texaco was forced back to the Texas Supreme Court for a review of the damage award.

The Texas Supreme Court upheld the verdict and affirmed the compensatory damages of $7.53 billion. It did, however, reduce the punitive damages from $3 billion to $1 billion, giving a total award of $8.53 billion. Including the interest that had accrued to that date, Texaco then owed Pennzoil $10.3 billion. Texaco's hopes now hinged on the U.S. Supreme Court.

On April 6, 1987, the U.S. Supreme Court invalidated the findings of the federal court regarding the bond issue. The Supreme Court found that the district court had impermissibly interfered in a matter properly left to the state court in Texas. At this point, Texaco was once again required to post the approximately $11 billion bond in order to pursue its other appeals (Bainbridge 1987, 110).

TEXACO'S NETWORK REACTS

Texaco found itself under increasing pressure from its creditors and suppliers to reach some sort of settlement with

Pennzoil. On April 8, two days after the Supreme Court verdict on the bond issue, several banks notified Texaco that they would not provide any additional funds to the company. Texaco had numerous active credit lines with banks, but many of these credit agreements contained clauses that allowed the banks to refuse to provide the money if the company's financial position changed "substantially." Manufacturers Hanover Trust activated such a clause when it canceled Texaco's $750 million line of credit days after the Supreme Court decision (*Business Week*, April 27, 1987, 102; *Time*, April 20, 1987, 50).

According to an affidavit Texaco would later file with the bankruptcy court, "Over 50 companies and banks told the company they were worried about [Texaco's] financial condition and wanted to alter their relationships" (debtor affidavit, *In re* Texaco Inc. 84 B.R. 893 [Bankr. S.D.N.Y. 1988]). Major suppliers, including Citgo and Occidental Petroleum, either threatened to stop doing business with Texaco or insisted on prepayment. Bank of America refused to wire funds to the company. Manufacturers Hanover, Chase Manhattan, and Morgan Guaranty demanded that the company maintain substantial cash balances with them. Unsecured borrowing was unavailable, and even secured financing was uncertain (see *Business Week*, April 27, 1987, 102; debtor affidavit, *In re* Texaco Inc. [1988]; *Oil Daily*, April 14, 1987, 1).

The *New York Times* reported that some of Texaco's leading lenders and business partners denied trying to alter their relationships with Texaco. However, a bankruptcy lawyer at Millibank, Tweed in New York looked skeptically at these denials: "I don't think that anyone would want to claim responsibility for having pushed Texaco into filing for bankruptcy" (*NYT*, April 23, 1987, D5).

Despite the pressure from the banks, Pennzoil and Texaco remained several billions of dollars apart in their negotiations. On April 8, 1987, several banks notified Texaco that they would no longer provide funds to the company. Chase Manhattan demanded that Texaco maintain new minimum balances in its accounts before the bank would transfer funds to satisfy commercial obligations. Three days later, on April 12, 1987, Texaco filed for Chapter 11 of the U.S. Bankruptcy Code. The bankruptcy was by far the largest in history.

THE TEXACO BANKRUPTCY

Most observers agreed that Texaco entered Chapter 11 bankruptcy in order to avoid paying the $10.53 billion award or posting the bond to cover the award. However, these observers missed the important role played by Texaco's lenders in this strategy. Texaco's lenders were anxious for a settlement to the case in order to remove the uncertainty now attached to their loans. Texaco hoped that by declaring bankruptcy, it would force Pennzoil into settling for something less than the original damages. Pennzoil's chief, Hugh Liedtke, said that he had been confronted with an attitude on the part of Texaco of either "you do what we say or we'll hold our breath till we die" (*NYT*, April 14, 1987, D1). Texaco confirmed Liedtke's perception when its trial counsel, Richard Miller, referred to the bankruptcy as a "bet-your-company" case, implying that Texaco had decided to take the gamble of throwing the company into bankruptcy in hopes of reducing the damage award (Bainbridge 1987, 111).

"Texaco can't frighten anyone into settling by declaring bankruptcy," Liedtke countered (*Time*, April 27, 1987, 52). Pennzoil accused Texaco of "improper use" of the bankruptcy code and said that Texaco had shown "arrogance and disregard for the whole judicial process" and was attempting "to use the bankruptcy laws improperly" (*NYT*, April 13, 1987, A1). Baine Kerr, Pennzoil's chief negotiator in the case, said that Texaco was simply using bankruptcy "for some tactical purpose that has nothing to do with the type of problem that bankruptcy laws are there to deal with" (ibid.). Interviewed on the "MacNeil-Lehrer Newshour," Liedtke bluntly stated his reasons for seeing the Texaco filing as a ploy: "The appraised net worth of Texaco ... is in the range of $23 to $26 billion.

. . . It certainly seems to me that $26 billion ought to be able to cover $12 [billion]" (as quoted in Petzinger 1987, 441).

Only Texaco's principal holding company and two financial subsidiaries actually filed for Chapter 11. This tactical move by Texaco allowed dozens of operating subsidiaries to carry on business as usual and alert their suppliers that they were not actually in bankruptcy. This move also gave Texaco the chance to argue that not all of its assets were available to creditors in the bankruptcy court.[3] "I thought that when we were suing Texaco, we were suing all of Texaco," Liedtke fumed (*Time*, April 27, 1987, 53).

Bankruptcy law immediately granted Texaco relief from having to post the supersedeas bond or pay Pennzoil the judgment award from the Houston case. The Chapter 11 filing simply put Pennzoil in the queue with all the other Texaco creditors. However, it was not just Pennzoil that charged a misuse of the bankruptcy process. A wide array of voices rang out intimating that Texaco was not really a "bankrupt" company but had declared bankruptcy as a "strategic" move. The following quotations indicate how far we have come both from the medieval notion of the bankrupt as a moral scoundrel that I detailed in chapter 1 *and* from the economic functionalist notion that bankruptcy is a last resort that managers accept when presented with indisputable economic data:

> "Much like Manville, . . . Texaco is using bankruptcy laws to buy time." (*Business Week*, April 27, 1987, 102)
> "Some legal observers believe that Texaco's goal is to extract a smaller judgment from Houston's district court . . . or to pressure Pennzoil into settling out of court for a fraction of the award." (*Business Week*, December 9, 1985, 36)
> "Texaco has bought time. Its prospects aren't as bleak." (Oil analyst at Shearson Lehman, quoted in *Business Week*, April 27, 1988, 52)

---

3. This issue, however, was never raised in court since a reorganization plan was soon agreed to by all parties.

"It seemed to many that [Texaco] had suddenly gained the upper hand in the high-stakes brawl it had appeared to be losing." (*Business Week,* April 27, 1988, 52)

"The U.S. was faced with the spectacle of a healthy corporation sheltering under laws ostensibly intended for the weak and the ailing." (*Time,* April 27, 1988)

Texaco declared bankruptcy "in order to forestall the enforcement of a $10.53 billion judgment against it." (*WSJ,* October 5, 1987, 6)

Even Texaco admitted that the bankruptcy filing was mainly a strategic effort to delay paying the Pennzoil court award: "Texaco's thousands of shareholders, as well as its public and private debtholders, have a substantial interest in the Texaco enterprise. Chapter 11 is the only way in which these interests can be protected, preserved and maximized in the face of the devastating effect of the Pennzoil judgment, particularly while that judgment is on appeal" (*Business Week,* April 27, 1987, 106).

In addition, Texaco indicated that if a settlement were reached or a large reduction in the bond granted, the company could withdraw or suspend the bankruptcy filing. "In other words, Texaco could be using its bankruptcy as the ultimate pressure tactic against Pennzoil" (*Time,* April 20, 1987, 50).

Texaco had assets in the neighborhood of $38 billion and liabilities of a little more than $24 billion, leaving the company with equity of approximately $13 billion—enough to pay the Pennzoil award. Court testimony showed that the firm had a liquidation value of anywhere between $22 and $26 billion (Texaco v. Pennzoil, 784 F.2d 1155). Texaco's favorable balance sheet left many performing "linguistic contortions" trying to explain why the company was in bankruptcy:

"You don't have to wait until you are too broke to reorganize." (bankruptcy expert with Latham & Watkins, quoted in *NYT,* April 14, 1987, d1)

"Under current bankruptcy law, bankruptcy doesn't necessarily mean broke." (*Business Week*, April 27, 1987, 102)
"This is not a bankruptcy as it would have been twenty years
ago. It's not like a company running out of money and can't
afford to pay their bills." (CEO of Cameron Iron Works, a
major Texaco supplier, quoted in *NYT*, April 13, 1987, A1)
"Its biggest trading partners know that it has a strong cash
flow . . . and, in reality, is solvent." (*Economist*, April 18,
1987, 64)
"If they were truly bankrupt they maybe wouldn't have
enough assets to pay off their debts." (Pennzoil negotiator
Baine Kerr, quoted in *NYT*, April 13, 1987, A1)
"While Texaco will be in bankruptcy, Texaco won't be a
bankrupt company." (oil analyst at the investment firm of
Tucker, Anthony & R. L. Day, quoted in *Time*, April 27,
1987, 52)

The apparent health of Texaco and the fact that it probably had enough equity to pay the award led people to see
that the company was not "broke." Investment bankers, supposedly expert arbiters of corporate health, saw the Texaco
bankruptcy for what it was: a strategic move to affect negotiations with Pennzoil. It was true that the company did not
have the liquid assets to pay off the award and would be
forced to sell major parts of its business. As a result, the
same people who realized it was *financially possible* to pay
the award recognized that such a payment would cause great
economic pain to Texaco. This led to a willingness to accept
new distinctions such as "broke" but not "too broke"; "in
bankruptcy" but "not bankrupt"; "bankrupt" but not "truly
bankrupt"; "in bankruptcy" but "in reality, solvent"; and
"bankrupt" but "not unable to pay the bills." These distinctions were made for a large corporation but would not be
made for an indigent individual.

All of the analysts who accused Texaco of misusing the
bankruptcy process underplayed the fact that commercial
lenders were parties to this strategic decision-making and
had in fact precipitated the bankruptcy filing by cutting off

loans and credit lines and requiring minimum cash balances. This effectively cut off Texaco's access to the appeals process, since it could not continue in business with these constraints. These actions severely constrained Texaco's options. A Texaco spokesperson said, "Texaco's ability to conduct operations had been threatened by companies and banks wanting to impose restrictive credit terms" (*NYT*, April 23, 1987, D5). The banks' refusal to provide loan capital, along with the unfavorable Supreme Court decision on the supersedeas bond issue, led to Texaco's strategic choice to file for bankruptcy. "The pressure became too great and we did what we had to do," said Texaco's president, James Kinnear (*Business Week*, April 27, 1987, 102). Texaco made the strategic choice to declare bankruptcy, but it did so in a highly constrained environment.

The very act of filing the bankruptcy petition gave Texaco new leverage. Texaco was granted a "stay" of the bond order, immediately putting Pennzoil in a waiting line with all other creditors. Texaco could now halt its payments of $2.5 million per day into an escrow account to cover the interest on the Houston judgment and stop its annual interest payments of $630 million on its $7 billion in routine business debt (*Petroleum Economist*, May 1987, 159). Of course, Texaco paid something in return for this. The company was now in bankruptcy court, and its operations would come under scrutiny by the court, as well as by creditors' and shareholders' committees.

After its initial shock at the Texaco filing, Pennzoil realized that it had better return to the business of negotiating a settlement with Texaco. If Pennzoil failed at this, it would face the prospect of waiting several years for a bankruptcy court settlement. Pennzoil was now in a position similar to that of the asbestos victims in the Manville bankruptcy. It had to weigh the advantages of taking a smaller amount of money now against the chance of a larger award after a great deal of legal wrangling. Bankruptcy in each case gave the debtor company new leverage.

Several days after Texaco announced its Chapter 11 filing, the company offered to pay Pennzoil $2 billion to settle the Getty case. Pennzoil countered by asking $3 to $5 billion, leaving the two sides still a considerable distance apart. However, the gap had closed a bit.

On June 30, 1987, Texaco received word that the Securities and Exchange Commission would file a brief in the Texaco appeal arguing that Pennzoil had broken SEC rules in its unsuccessful takeover attempt of Getty. Recall that Texaco had maintained that Pennzoil had gone "outside the tender offer" by first announcing a public offer for 20 percent of Getty at $100 per share and then privately negotiating with Getty to acquire 42 percent of the stock at $112.50. The SEC brief argued that this indeed violated its Rule 10b-13. This gave Texaco a big boost in its position but moved the sides further apart, since Texaco became less anxious to settle with Pennzoil because its chances of overturning the entire damage award had drastically improved (*Oil Daily*, July 1, 1987, 1; *Los Angeles Times*, June 30, 1987, sec. 4: 1). Several months passed with little progress being made in the negotiations between the two oil companies. There was some indication that Texaco's creditors and shareholders were becoming impatient with the speed of the bankruptcy process. "Various outsiders are becoming impatient," an oil industry analyst warned (*NYT*, November 18, 1987, D6).

Meanwhile, in the bankruptcy court, the various parties were arguing over whether Pennzoil, as Texaco's major creditor, should be allowed to inspect Texaco's financial records. Texaco sought to block the action based on the fact that Pennzoil, a major competitor, would gain access to corporate secrets (Pennzoil eventually won limited access).

As of November 1987, Texaco had still not proposed a reorganization plan. The creditors' committee, representing Texaco's major creditors and lenders, became active in trying to mediate the Texaco-Pennzoil dispute. The committee proposed a "base and cap" plan intended to allow the two warring sides to continue the appeals process while bringing Texaco out of bankruptcy. This plan called for the two sides to agree to a "base" figure and a "cap" figure. Texaco would pay the base amount immediately, and Pennzoil would keep that amount regardless of the outcome of the appeals. In return, Pennzoil would only be able to collect up to the "cap" amount if it eventually won on appeal. This strategy, however, simply gave the companies two figures to argue over rather than one. Texaco offered a base of $400,000 and a cap of $2 billion. Pennzoil countered with a base of $1.5 billion and a cap of $5 billion. The two sides seemed even further apart.

ENTER CARL ICAHN

During the final week of November 1987, seven months after Texaco declared bankruptcy, financier and takeover specialist Carl Icahn acquired a large chunk of Texaco stock from another large investor, Robert Holmes à Court. The purchase raised Icahn's stake in Texaco from 2.4 to 12.3 percent, thrusting Icahn into the center of the bankruptcy battle as the holder of the largest single block of Texaco stock. Several days later, Icahn's lawyer, David Friedman, made his initial appearance in the bankruptcy court of Judge Howard Schwartzberg in the following exchange:

Friedman: We offer a new face.

Schwartzberg: Is he [Icahn] the hero we've been looking for?

Friedman: Maybe, maybe not.

This exchange reflected Judge Schwartzberg's growing desire to see Texaco and Pennzoil settle the case without going through a drawn-out battle over competing reorganization plans. Icahn rapidly became a dominant force on the shareholders' committee and greatly enhanced the power of that committee. Icahn and the institutional investors were eager for a settlement because the lengthy legal battle was draining Texaco's resources (institutional investors, taken together, held 35 percent of Texaco stock, with Icahn holding 12.3 percent and Kohlberg, Kravis, Roberts nearly 5 percent). Texaco management, however, felt that it should fight on in the appeals process in hopes of reducing the settlement.

In December 1987, Texaco's period of exclusivity was drawing to a close. Up until this time, the debtor (Texaco) was the only party allowed to file a reorganization plan. Texaco did not appear ready to do this and asked for an extension of the exclusivity period. In a major turning point in the case, Judge Schwartzberg extended the exclusivity period for forty days, but also ruled that if the creditors, shareholders, and Pennzoil agreed to a plan, he would consider it despite Texaco's exclusivity. "[I] tried to put pressure on all sides to negotiate, and not be posturing," Schwartzberg would later say (*NYT*, December 20, 1987, A36). The judge's plan worked, and the decision set off furious negotiations among the various parties (*Oil Daily*, July 27, 1988, 10).

On December 2, there were reports that the creditors' committee was trying to put together its own plan in hopes of getting the shareholders and Pennzoil to agree and then invoking the "cram down" mechanism of the bankruptcy code to force the plan on Texaco (recall that the "cram down" provision allows the judge to approve a plan notwithstanding the protests of the debtor if all of the other parties agree to the plan). The shareholders' committee, led by Icahn, also began negotiating with Pennzoil directly, thereby bypassing Texaco management. A bankruptcy expert argued that "in these newer, bigger cases, with companies that are arguably solvent, it's natural that shareholders would become more aggressive" (*WSJ*, January 21, 1988, 1).

The general creditors' committee seemed to have played a major role in trying to negotiate a deal without the presence of Texaco management. A New York bankruptcy attorney argued that "there has been an unprecedented usurpation of power by the creditors' committee. . . . I know of no situation where the committee usurped the function of the debtor in negotiating a settlement" (*NYT*, December 19, 1987, 44).

By December 12, the shareholders, creditors, and Pennzoil had agreed on a figure of $3 billion. The action by the shareholders' committee outraged Texaco's president, James Kinnear. Later, Kinnear would maintain that he could have negotiated a more favorable settlement for Texaco if his own shareholders had not bypassed management.

The agreement by the three parties put enormous pressure on Texaco, since the company knew that Schwartzberg was likely to allow the filing of a plan agreed to by these three parties. Texaco feared that the plan would be forced upon it through the "cram down" rules. Texaco entered marathon discussions with Pennzoil on December 17, and by the 18th of December the two oil giants had an agreement in principle on the $3 billion figure. Texaco filed a reorganization plan based on the agreement on December 21, 1987, thereby ending the largest bankruptcy in history.

THE BANKRUPTCY PLAN

Under the agreement, Texaco would pay Pennzoil $3 billion to end the dispute that began as a takeover battle for Getty Oil. Although considerably lower than the original award, the settlement still was eleven times greater than any court judgment ever sustained on appeal. The business press pointed out that Pennzoil's president, Hugh Liedtke, could use the $3 billion to buy the World Trade Center and the RCA building if he wanted real estate, every team in the National Football League if he fancied sports, or all the existing Rembrandts and Picassos if he wanted to dabble in artwork (*NYT*, March 24, 1988, D9).

When Liedtke was finally wired the money in April 1988, it had to be sent across telephone lines in several chunks, since the Federal Reserve's computer system was limited to $999,999,999.99. Liedtke apparently decided to hold off on buying every team in the NFL, and instead put the money into money market instruments. The amount was so large that Liedtke was advised by money managers to borrow money in the weeks before receiving the $3 billion so that he could invest the money gradually. If he invested the $3 billion all at once, he alone could drive the nation's money market rates down considerably, causing market tumult.

Texaco's other creditors, including the major banks with loans to the company, received 100 percent of what they were owed, plus interest. They also began loaning money to Texaco as part of the reorganization, but now the loans were on the bank's terms. A group of between twenty and thirty international and domestic banks stepped forward with a $3 billion bridge loan to pay the settlement. Texaco was now using the "consortium lending" that it had managed to avoid in its earlier, more powerful days. The banks included some very restrictive covenants in the agreement that allowed them to pull the loan if any one investor acquired 30 percent or more of the shares of Texaco. A second covenant stipulated that if Texaco were taken over and its credit rating downgraded, the creditors would be allowed to sell their notes back to the company. Yet another covenant limited Texaco's debt to from 60 to 65 percent of equity. The lenders had gained many of the restrictions they had never before been able to place on Texaco.

The $3 billion loan allowed Texaco to come up with a strategy to sell off assets gradually. The company certainly had the assets to pay the $3 billion. The bankers provided the loan at competitive rates, presumably making the payment of the award both "financially possible" and "financially practicable."

In March 1988, Moody's reviewed Texaco debt for possible upgrading and Standard & Poor's upgraded it to a more respectable BBB+ and removed the company from its "CreditWatch" list. These actions would make it easier for the firm to borrow money once again and lower the cost of borrowing. The company began developing plans to reenter the commercial paper market (*WSJ*, April 18, 1988, 2).

Texaco would never get to argue its objections to the original award in any higher court. CEO Kinnear continued to feel that he could have gotten a better deal for Texaco, but he vowed to restructure the company. Icahn made a paper profit of $143 million dollars and was about to embark on a long, unsuccessful proxy battle for control of Texaco.

BANKRUPTCY AS LEVERAGE

Like Manville and Continental, Texaco used a bankruptcy filing to gain strategic advantage. The $10.53 billion judgment in the Texas courtroom had introduced huge strains into Texaco's relations with its lenders, suppliers, and employees. Texaco chose to enter the bankruptcy process in a strategic attempt to reduce that strain by eliminating or reducing the damage award to Pennzoil.

Texaco was successful to a limited degree. The bankruptcy process provided several advantages to Texaco management. First, it bought time in order for Texaco to pursue its numerous appeals. Texaco originally hoped that it would have the protection of the bankruptcy court long enough to argue its case up to the Supreme Court if necessary. Second, by filing for bankruptcy, Pennzoil was placed in line with all other creditors and could no longer use the $11 billion supersedeas bond as a club against Texaco, since the bond was "stayed" pending a reorganization plan. Third, the bankruptcy filing allowed Texaco to discontinue paying interest on all of its other commercial loans. Once the creditors stopped receiving interest payments on existing loans, they could be expected to step up the pressure on both Pennzoil and Texaco to reach a settlement, which would surely be lower than the original award.

When Texaco made the strategic decision to declare bankruptcy, its choice was limited to a set of options resulting from the actions of various other players in the case. These actions precipitated the crisis that led to the bankruptcy filing. Some commentators have argued that Texaco chose bankruptcy, but they have missed the important role that financial institutions played in limiting Texaco's options prior to the bankruptcy filing. Several major institutions made choices owing to their past social relations with Texaco as well as to economic and legal judgments regarding the company's current and future state.

The Houston court judgment altered many of Texaco's formerly stable relationships. The company's debt rating was lowered, making it extremely costly for the firm to raise money in financial markets. Banks refused to provide unsecured loans, and Texaco found it difficult to arrange secured loans. Texaco also faced almost immediate restrictions on its ability to move money within its own accounts.

These actions were not solely owing to the Houston verdict. Lenders also seem to have been operating on the basis of past relations with Texaco, which had been stormy to say the least. In the past, Texaco had refused to allow a lead bank to arrange consortium financing, instead preferring to put together its own financing syndicates, thereby avoiding restrictive terms. As a result, the major banks did not seem willing to step in and help Texaco weather the crisis. Lenders saw an opportunity to install the consortium financing and loan restrictions that it had been unable to place on Texaco in the past.

Although Texaco achieved a favorable ruling in the New York court, it was soon overturned and the firm's lenders again reacted swiftly. Manufacturers Hanover canceled Texaco's credit line, and many other banks attempted to cancel or place restrictions on Texaco's credit.

Some of Texaco's suppliers also placed pressure on the company by demanding payment in advance, although this seemed to be less decisive in Texaco's decision to declare bankruptcy than the lenders' actions. The loss of supplier and customer confidence is a longer-term business problem, while the lack of capital proved to be an *immediate* problem. In other words, large lenders have greater and more immediate power to constrain choices. Major banks are in a more centralized position than suppliers. Their control over capital is one of the bases of power that may be external to the bankruptcy arena, but provides lenders with tremendous advantage in fashioning a settlement in their favor.

Given this constrained environment, bankruptcy was a method for Texaco to alter its crucial, troubling relationships with Pennzoil, creditors, and suppliers, something it was clearly unable to do outside of bankruptcy. Most important, Chapter 11 stopped Pennzoil from attempting to collect the $11 billion judgment and encouraged it to settle for a lower amount rather than wait while Texaco "held its breath." Once the award was lowered, Texaco was once again able to borrow from the major banks, although this time with numerous restrictive covenants.

Not only was the bankruptcy process socially constructed by the major institutions in the case, but several crucial legal interpretations involved important social-political considerations. These sociological elements demonstrate the concrete importance of the embeddedness of law in the social world. Although such legal constructs as "contracts" are sometimes seen as residing in the realm of "natural rights," it is clear that they have strong grounding in society. For example, the definition of a "contract" in this case can only be understood in terms of the social context set by the Pennzoil legal team. Pennzoil argued that a handshake and an agreement in principle were enough to form a contract, while Texaco argued that a formal agreement was necessary. In the original trial, Pennzoil's lawyers successfully painted the case as a battle between a hometown, "good ol' boy" company and a corporate giant dominated by "Yankee Wall Street Types." Pennzoil succeeded in convincing the Houston jury that, in Texas, a handshake was as good as any formal legal document "drafted by a bunch of lawyers." Thus, the perceived social conventions of what it meant to "do business in Texas" were absolutely crucial to the determination of the existence of a contract in this case. The definition of a contract in turn was crucial to the determination of Texaco's liability. If the court had sided with Texaco's version of what constitutes a contract, it might have had absolutely no liability for damages.

This case once again illustrates the importance in the reduction in stigma attached to bankruptcy and demonstrates the beginnings of linguistic distinctions to grapple with the distinction between a company that is "bankrupt, but not really broke." Again, a key aspect of the bankruptcy was the manufacture of the claim to bankrupt status. In this case the key question became not only "How are liabilities defined?" but also "When does a liability become an 'official liability'?"—that is, one recognized by other important players as "real."

The calculation of damages demonstrated the non-technical, political, and socially embedded nature of estimating non-concrete liabilities. A jury in Houston arrived at a damage award of $10.53 billion, while an appellate judge in New York arrived at a figure of $1 billion. The bankruptcy of the nation's third largest oil company rested on a liability that could differ by a factor of ten, depending on who was doing the calculation.

When liabilities can differ so greatly, we must look to sociological reasons. The Houston jury accepted Pennzoil's interpretation of damages, perhaps because it was the only interpretation they were presented with, and did not face the question of the breakup of Texaco. Individual jurors might not feel the same pressure to prevent the breakup of a large company as a federal judge. Judge Brieant's interpretation of damages seemed driven as much by the desire to allow Texaco to appeal the case and avoid the breakup of the company as by any technical superiority in estimating the damages related to the lost Getty oil.

The supersedeas bond requirement in Texas law prevented Texaco from pursuing additional appeals of its case. As in many aspects of law, the locale in which the case was tried became crucial to the outcome. If the original Texaco-Pennzoil dispute had occurred in a place without this type of bond requirement, or where the bond could have been covered by unliquidated assets, Texaco would have continued its appeals for several years. But the Texas bond requirement gave Pennzoil an enormous club with which to discourage Texaco from its appeals. In order to appeal, Texaco would have had to sell huge chunks of its businesses.

Whether Texaco ever belonged in bankruptcy remains a contentious issue. Some analysts have argued that Texaco's filing was indeed proper. Frank Kennedy, professor of law at the University of Michigan Law School and the executive director of the commission that drafted the current bankruptcy code, believes that Texaco's filing was "entirely consistent with the legislative purpose of the federal code" and that "the question is whether there is a real debtor-creditor problem" (Bainbridge 1987, 114).

Texaco had a "debtor-creditor problem," of course, but the real question is not whether there was a problem but whether it resulted in a "bankrupt" company. The answer to this question, I think, depends on the assumptions one makes about the purpose of the bankruptcy code. If the code exists to preserve the capital of a corporation and avoid the economic upset of forcing the closing of oil rigs and gasoline stations, or the large-scale selling of assets, then the bankruptcy process worked properly. If, however, the purpose of the code is to provide a neutral forum for the collection of debts by creditors and, more broadly, as a mechanism to ensure economic efficiency, then it is difficult to see how the process operated appropriately in this case. Little testimony in the case related to the efficiency of the company. The court seemed less interested in the incredibly complex question of whether the firm would be worth more broken up or kept together than in getting the two warring sides to settle their differences. If we accept for the moment that the $10.53 billion award was a proper liability (i.e., an accurate assessment of damages) and that the Houston jury had a legitimate right to come to such a verdict, then a mechanism designed to ensure an efficient national economy must treat it as a proper liability in its estimation of the efficiency of Texaco. But, instead, the award was treated throughout the case as "incorrect," "absurd," and a bargaining chip. Many of Judge Schwartzberg's decisions in the bankruptcy case were aimed at pressuring the two sides to negotiate a reduced settlement. This case thus became the logical extension of the trends outlined in chapter 1. All involved, with the possible exception of Pennzoil, seemed to rule out the breakup of the nation's third largest oil company from the outset.

By most accounts, Texaco could have paid the original damage award to Pennzoil, although that would have entailed selling off large parts of the company. The company itself argued that it had the assets to back up the damage award to Pennzoil while it appealed the case. Texaco maintained that it simply did not want to liquidate those assets, possibly causing harm to employees, shareholders, and management. However, it is not immediately apparent that a sell-off would have caused harm to shareholders and employees. A case can also be made for a spin-off of assets to smaller, regional companies *helping* shareholders and employees. It was Texaco management that would clearly lose if there was a sell-off of assets. One can't help but wonder whether, if a smaller company had made the blunder Texaco made in the Getty takeover, it would have been as protected as Texaco.

By arguing that the payment of the award was "financially impracticable," Texaco was able to mobilize the bankruptcy process, giving it the upper hand for the first time against Pennzoil. Many of the players involved accepted the standard of "financial impracticability" rather than risk the breakup of Texaco. This case illustrates the courts' reluctance to break up large companies and raises questions about whether bankruptcy really operates as a weeding-out mechanism as described in most "survival of the fittest" and "creative destruction" models.

If the main aim of the bankruptcy process in large cases is to preserve private capital and keep large companies together, then the process may not be able to ensure overall economic efficiency by acting as a technical, neutral arbiter between companies allowed to reorganize and companies forced to liquidate.

6

Bankruptcy as Strategy: Avoiding Financial Burden and Shifting Financial Risk

> Bankruptcy court is becoming a court of first resort rather than last.
>
> —*Martin Klein, a bankruptcy attorney*

> Most things in life . . . are important only to those that have them. Money, in contrast, is equally important to those who have it and those who don't.
>
> —*John Kenneth Galbraith,* Money

THE MOBILIZATION OF BANKRUPTCY LAW

Several researchers have found that people often invoke the legal process to achieve goals never predicated by doctrinal views of the law (Mayhew 1975; Zemans 1982). For example, one might sue a neighbor simply for revenge—to tarnish that person's reputation or to force him or her to spend resources in self-defense. Not surprisingly, these studies have found that the ability of individuals to mobilize the legal process is affected by power, socioeconomic status, legal socialization, education, and a host of other factors (Zemans 1982 and 1983).

We can say the same thing about organizations' use of bankruptcy. Companies and commercial creditors can invoke the bankruptcy process for a wide variety of reasons, many of which do not conform to doctrinal or economic pre-

160

dictions. As I have shown, a firm may choose bankruptcy to forestall lawsuits and force a compensation system in place of the tort system, to eliminate union contracts, or to reduce a court award in a corporate takeover battle.

Firms might also choose bankruptcy to force the government to take over responsibility for a pension plan or health care coverage promised to retirees, to avoid cleaning up a toxic waste site, to alter a bargaining relationship, or even for revenge against a competitor. Organizations with greater resources, superior public relations and legal knowledge, and access to legal and financial specialists are able to use bankruptcy more easily than organizations or individuals without these resources.

The cases I have chosen to call "strategic bankruptcies" exhibit three key elements. First, the firm declares bankruptcy to pursue a limited organizational or political goal that it had unsuccessfully pursued outside of the bankruptcy arena. Second, the firm (and perhaps some of the firm's creditors) actively shape the claim to bankruptcy through strategic actions (e.g., recording liabilities on a balance sheet after years of fighting to keep them off it, or shifting assets from one corporate unit to another). Alternative definitions of the firm's financial condition are readily available (i.e., the firm could be plausibly defined as "not bankrupt" as well) but are not chosen. Finally, these cases involve innovative legal strategies aimed at legitimating the firm's claim to bankruptcy. Novel legal arguments and court decisions are made to extend bankruptcy relief to new, uncharted areas. Through this broadening, larger societal issues are brought into the bankruptcy forum.

Are strategic bankruptcies different from other business bankruptcies? I think these cases fall at the end of a continuum of business bankruptcy cases rather than being a distinct type. At one extreme of the continuum are firms with a single concrete, indisputable liability and a single concrete, indisputable asset. There is thus little debate over the assets and liabilities of the firm and hence little strategic action to shape the claim to bankruptcy. At the other end of the continuum are firms with very vague, arguable liabilities (e.g., contestable damage awards such as future asbestos liabilities; non-concrete costs associated with labor contracts, such as seniority provisions and work rules) and vague, arguable assets (e.g., patents, inventions, products with high risk/return potential, firm value attached mainly to company name and reputation rather than to actual products). These cases are ripe for what I call the "social construction of bankruptcy": efforts at shaping assets and liabilities to coincide with the interests of the parties doing the shaping. It is at this end of the continuum that we are likely to find strategic bankruptcies.

Earlier we saw that the dominant theories of corporate bankruptcy cling to an economic functionalist stance by assuming that managers have no choice when they enter Chapter 11. The interorganizational and institutional analyses I have applied to three of the most important recent bankruptcy cases suggest that bankruptcy is often not a passive reaction to economic imperatives.

In this final chapter, I wish to suggest a new way of thinking about bankruptcy. Rather than viewing it as a punishment, a neutral debt-collection system, or a market mechanism to ensure nationwide efficiency, I prefer to think of the bankruptcy process as a political arena in which organizations invoke bankruptcy to avoid current financial burdens and shift future financial risk to other, more vulnerable parties. In this chapter, I shall outline my alternative to dominant theories of bankruptcy and illustrate how and why organizations use bankruptcy as a strategy. I shall then assess the implications of my theory for the dominant theories of business bankruptcy.

ORGANIZATIONAL CONSTRUCTION OF THE BOTTOM LINE

In the Manville, Continental, and Texaco cases, a variety of organizations tried to shape the financial data that led to the designation "bankrupt." These three cases illustrate some of the mechanisms of what I call the "organizational construction of the bottom line." These cases show the folly of bankruptcy theorists' willing acceptance of balance-sheet figures as the only objective depiction of a firm's financial state. All the following mechanisms were employed in these cases as organizations tried to construct the bottom line to suit their interests. Because all of the dominant theories assume that all parties want to *avoid* bankruptcy, they often fail to see these efforts aimed at *gaining* the designation "bankrupt."

Defining Assets and Liabilities

The first way in which the claim to bankruptcy may be shaped is in the control of the definition of seemingly technical terms such as *asset* and *liability*. For example, Manville chose not to estimate its asbestos liabilities for several years running in the late 1970s and early 1980s. A footnote in the annual report exempted Manville from registering future liabilities on its balance sheet, since the company maintained that these liabilities were inestimable. Thus by controlling when a liability became official, management could define the firm as "not bankrupt." However, weeks before its 1982 Chapter 11 filing, the company reversed course and chose to commission estimates of future asbestos liabilities. Suddenly the firm had an "official liability" of $2 billion and declared bankruptcy.

The actual damage that would lead to these future lawsuits, of course, occurred many years before the 1982 bankruptcy filing. The firm's asbestos liabilities were as real in 1980 as they were in 1982. However, choices were made to keep this amount off the balance sheet through 1981 and to put it on the balance sheet in 1982. The claim to bankruptcy was constructed by controlling the designation of "official liabilities." Manville's designation as "bankrupt" thus resulted from strategic action rather than adaptation to balance-sheet data and market conditions.

Defining the "Bankrupt Unit"

The claim to bankruptcy can also be manufactured by controlling the definition of the "bankrupt unit." In strategic bankruptcies, the claim to bankrupt status is often constructed by designating only a part of the company as bankrupt. Texas Air owned 90 percent of Continental, and the two had engaged in numerous business transactions indicating that Continental was a subsidiary. Yet Continental chose to exclude Texas Air from its Chapter 11 filing, thereby eliminating the parent company's substantial assets from court consideration. If Continental *had* included Texas Air in its bankruptcy filing, the bankruptcy petition might have been thrown out of court on the grounds that the company was not insolvent and was filing "in bad faith." Similarly, Texaco carefully chose which part of the company it would define as the "bankrupt unit," including only the holding company and two financial subsidiaries. This allowed numerous operating companies to promise suppliers and creditors that they would carry on "business as usual." Ability to define the bankrupt unit is thus crucial both in legitimating the claim to bankruptcy and in shaping the assets available to creditors in the bankruptcy arena.

Shifting Assets from a "Bankrupt Unit" to a "Non-bankrupt Unit"

Another mechanism for shaping the claim to bankruptcy is shifting assets from a corporate unit defined as "bankrupt" to other units designated as "not bankrupt." Continental's movement of assets to its parent company just prior to the Chapter 11 filing illustrates the strategic nature of shaping assets and liabilities in preparation for bankruptcy. Offering public stock in Continental also helped legitimate the claim that it was a separate unit from Texas Air. So shifting assets can both ensure the designation "bankrupt" and leave less money available to those with claims against the company.

Taking Action to Ensure Bankrupt Status

Management can also stake a claim to bankruptcy by taking actions *intended* to secure and legitimate the company's designation as bankrupt. For example, Continental's management chose continually to reduce its contract offer to unionized employees, prompting a strike. Continental could have continued to bargain with its unions in hopes of a turn-around or opted for the Employee Stock Ownership Plan (ESOP) proposed by its employees. At the time of the filing, the company still had cash and marketable securities of $58 million, $186 million in accounts receivable, and $44 million in receivables from affiliates. Instead, management took actions to ensure that the firm could gain access to Chapter 11. Once all the firm's unionized workers were on strike, the firm could justify its claim to "equity insolvency."

The Process of Company Valuation

Determining the value of a company constitutes yet another avenue for constructing a claim to bankruptcy. Throughout the bankruptcy process, company valuations are used to measure the current and future value of the firm. If a firm is judged to be worth more kept together than sold, the company is allowed to reorganize and continue in business. Despite its quasi-scientific quality, the valuation process can be easily manipulated. Firm value is generally determined by the equation $V = I/i$, where I = the typical annual earnings the reorganized entity can be expected to attain in the future and i = an appropriate capitalization rate for determining the present value of that earnings stream in perpetuity. As one legal analyst aptly commented, "The inescapable fact remains that the process involves solving an algebraic formula in which all of the elements are unknown. It is hardly surprising, then, that the valuation process . . . is at best a ballpark guess and at worst a wild figment of some expert's imagination" (Rosenberg 1975, 1186).

Rosenberg highlights the uncertainty attached to all the variables in the valuation equation. However, he makes the valuation process sound serendipitous, as if no organizational or individual actors have interests in the outcome. It is much more likely that different actors will pursue *particular* valuations that suit their interests. For example, an unsecured creditor might want a valuation high enough to be sure that its priority layer is paid in full, while shareholders want a valuation that is higher so as to give them a share of the firm's assets after all of the creditors are paid.

The bankruptcy court often uses valuations to determine whether a firm is to be liquidated or continue in business. This figure can, however, be drastically altered simply by changing the capitalization rate. Consider the following example (see Rosenberg 1975 for further details): If the annual earnings stream of a reorganized firm is predicted to be $100,000 (this estimate is in itself difficult to make) and you capitalize this amount at 10 percent, the current value of the firm is $1,000,000 ($100,000/.10). However, if you merely change the capitalization rate to 12 percent, you reduce the current value of the firm to only $833,333 ($100,000/.12). This is a dramatic difference in percentage terms (16.67 percent) and could easily prove decisive in whether the firm is forced to liquidate or is reorganized.

Thus, if you desire to make the firm appear solvent, you choose one capitalization rate; if you desire to make it appear insolvent, you choose another. As Rosenberg notes, "Predictably, suspicions arise that the actual process in many cases is the determination of the desired V [value], and that I [annual income stream] and i [capitalization rate] are filled in accordingly" (1975, 1186).

The inherent problem in predicting future income streams is highlighted by the fact that even the best investment advisors give contradictory advice on such estimates when recommending stock purchases. In all bankruptcy cases, estimating the current and future value of the company is a tricky process. This is even more so in "strategic bankruptcies," which center on arguments over highly uncertain future assets and debts. In the Manville and A. H. Robins cases, for example, asbestos liabilities and Dalkon Shield injuries respectively and company profitability had to be estimated for twenty to thirty years into the future.

Several bankruptcy judges have admitted just how arbitrary this process can seem, even to them. "I always have great misgivings because it [estimating future feasibility of the firm] requires some quality I don't possess to predict what is going to happen in five years. I don't think anyone can predict what is going to happen tomorrow, which makes this thing like Alice in Wonderland," said Judge Babbitt (quoted in Nelson 1981, 115).

In another bankruptcy case, this one requiring a valuation of oil that had *not yet* been found in a large parcel of Arctic land, the judge wrote in his judicial opinion:

> [To say] that you can appraise the values in the Canadian Arctic is to say that you can attend the County Fair with your crystal ball, because that is the only possible way you can come up with a result. . . . My final conclusion . . . is that it is worth somewhere between $90 million and $100 million as a going concern, and to satisfy the people that want precision on the value, I fix the exact amount at . . . $96,856,850, which of course is a total absurdity that anybody could fix a value with that degree of precision, but for the lawyers that want me to make that fool estimate, I have just made it. (Citibank v. Baer, 651 F.2d 1341, 1347 [10th Cir. 1980], quoted in Fortgang and Meyer 1985, 1131–32)

Legal and Linguistic Strategies

Novel legal and linguistic interpretations can also help to legitimate the claim to bankruptcy. The Texaco case was viewed so widely as a strategic maneuver that many dubbed it "the bet-your-company case." Texaco continually argued that paying the damages was *not* financially impossible, but rather "financially impracticable." In fact, Texaco itself argued in court immediately before its Chapter 11 filing that its assets were enough to pay the award, albeit at the expense of selling off large chunks of the company. At the time of the filing, Texaco had $35 billion in assets, annual revenues of $32 billion, and a healthy cash flow. The appraised net worth of the company was in the $23 to $26 billion range. As Pennzoil's CEO, Hugh Liedtke, stated, "It certainly seems to me that $26 billion ought to cover $12 [billion]" (Petzinger 1987, 441). Although Texaco could have paid the award, it chose Chapter 11 bankruptcy to improve its negotiating stance.

THE ROLE OF OTHER ORGANIZATIONS

It is clear, then, that management can shape the claim to bankruptcy. But the story does not end there. The evidence from these cases suggests a second challenge to conventional wisdom: Chapter 11 is employed as a strategy, not only by managers of ailing corporations, but also by other organizations attempting to gain strategic advantage. In these three cases, large commercial creditors played the most influential role in controlling the bankruptcy process. In each of the cases, a series of key questions were posed in court that went to the heart of whether the firm was indeed bankrupt and what value was available to creditors. These questions recurred in each of the strategic bankruptcies: What is a company? What is a liability? When does the liability become an "official liability"? What is the future value of the firm? Commercial creditors, more than any other institution or group, exercised considerable power in constructing the answers to these questions.

In the Manville case, commercial creditors played a pivotal role in constructing the claim to bankruptcy and in influencing the firm's behavior. To the lay observer, Manville appeared schizophrenic, saying one day that its asbestos liabilities were inestimable and the very next day providing an estimate. But once we examine the activities of Manville's lenders, the behavior makes sense. Morgan Guaranty, Manville's lead lender for decades, gradually became convinced that it stood a better chance of getting its money back with a Chapter 11 filing than by allowing Manville to fight individual claims in court. Morgan had a well-placed representative on Manville's board of directors. He spearheaded a drive to hire a new auditor, which in turn immediately approved an SEC filing estimating future asbestos liabilities for the very first time. This paved the way for the designation "bankrupt" and a Chapter 11 filing only weeks later.

An economic bankruptcy model would take Manville's balance-sheet figures, filed with the bankruptcy petition, and general market conditions at the time of the filing and conclude that Manville had no choice other than bankruptcy. Manville's balance sheet at the time of the filing clearly implied bankruptcy. But I have shown that choices were made by both the company and its lenders to shape the bottom line and gain access to bankruptcy. Manville's balance sheet made the company look quite healthy in the late 1970s and early 1980s, but in the bankruptcy filing, the balance sheet describes a company as having a $2 billion liability. While some journalists concluded that Manville management chose strategic bankruptcy to avoid liability, it is equally true to say that Manville's main lenders helped "choose" the bankruptcy. Manville's lenders constrained the firm's actions by threatening to speed up loan payments unless the firm quickly resolved its asbestos crisis. Morgan's representative on Manville's board appears to have been at the center of the firm's strategy.

Similarly, Texaco's lenders constrained the oil company's actions. After Texaco was hit with a $10.53 billion damage award, its bankers acted quickly by applying pressure to Texaco to force a settlement with Pennzoil. Texaco faced immediate restrictions on its ability to move money within its own accounts, and lenders introduced minimum cash balance requirements. In addition, Texaco found it impossible to locate new loan capital. These actions helped precipitate the strategic bankruptcy.

When Continental filed for Chapter 11 bankruptcy, commercial lenders supported the filing and did not join the unions in arguing that the firm was using bankruptcy as a strategy. Lender support continued through much of the bankruptcy process. For example, in order to keep the airline flying in the first crucial weeks of bankruptcy, commercial creditors backed the company's request to free up money that would normally be held in protection for creditors' claims. The lenders did finally split with management once they were sure that the company would survive bankruptcy. Lenders balked at the firm's third request to free up money to buy a fleet of new planes, arguing instead that leasing planes would suffice.

So there is strong evidence in each of these cases that other large organizations, most notably commercial creditors, are parties to this strategic decision-making. Large commercial creditors can exercise a significant amount of constraint in the bankruptcy process for several reasons. First, they usually dominate the creditors' committee, which is often composed of the largest creditors. As I detailed in chapter 1, the creditors' committee plays a crucial role in shaping the final reorganization plan. Changes in the 1978 Bankruptcy Reform Act gave the creditors' committee increased power over the bankruptcy process.

Large banks also have power outside of the formal bankruptcy process in that they control a universal commodity required by almost all firms: money. A firm is likely to be in desperate need of capital to emerge from bankruptcy. The number of institutions that can provide this capital is quite limited. By providing or withholding loans, banks can exercise considerable influence over the bankruptcy process. In each of the three cases, lenders at some point cut off access to capital and helped create the crisis leading to bankruptcy. In the Texaco case, lenders effectively blocked Texaco's ability to appeal its case further against Pennzoil by restricting credit lines. This turned the damage award into an official liability that Texaco had to deal with immediately to avoid restrictions on its capital.

When lenders decide to loan funds to a firm, they have a strong incentive to police this investment closely. They can accomplish this either through the presence of a board member or through restrictive loan covenants that require the bank to be repaid before other groups if the firm reenters bankruptcy.

In the Manville bankruptcy, Morgan Guaranty did both. A Morgan Guaranty board member became pivotal when he headed the effort to hire a new auditor to approve a new financial filing that made future asbestos liabilities an "official liability." Corporate directors, who may have very limited roles during times of corporate prosperity, can thus become pivotal figures in shaping business crises. In addition to having an influential board member in place, Morgan protected itself in preparation for a potential bankruptcy by including loan covenants on $100 million in notes that prohibited the incurrence of any secured debt that would be repaid before Morgan's loan (see Johns-Manville Corp. and Morgan Guaranty Trust of New York, Trustee, Indenture dated May 1, 1979; Roe 1984, 857). The largest lenders commonly use these covenants to protect their loans. Obviously, future asbestos victims did not have the power or opportunity to bargain for similar restrictions on the company that damaged their health.

As we have seen, commercial creditors can also exercise influence within the bankruptcy arena by supporting or opposing the release of restricted cash for use as operating capital. In the Continental case, lenders had to make the crucial decision of whether to support Continental through the first few weeks of its Chapter 11 case or to pull the plug and force liquidation to prevent further draining of capital. The lenders decided to side with Lorenzo's strategy to cut labor costs by supporting Continental's request to use restricted cash as operating capital and replace the restricted cash with new receivables not yet collected. The bankers' support allowed Continental to offer extremely low fares to woo customers who were trying to figure out whether buying tickets on Continental was worth the risk. By all accounts, these first few weeks were decisive in Continental surviving bankruptcy. The findings from these three major cases suggest that both management and the largest creditors are the most significant and powerful players in constructing the claim to bankruptcy.

BUT WHY CHOOSE BANKRUPTCY?

Even after reading my analyses of these cases, it may continue to be inconceivable to many that managers or commercial creditors would *choose* bankruptcy, given the cost to a firm's reputation, legal fees, and constraints on managerial discretion while under court scrutiny. In certain instances, however, Chapter 11 is chosen from a narrowed set of options. Chapter 11 bankruptcy in these cases provides companies and creditors with the opportunity to attempt "network surgery"; to transform troublesome ties with other organizations in ways that might not be possible outside of bankruptcy. Through bankruptcy, organizations try to avoid current financial burdens and shift future financial risk to more vulnerable parties.

In the Continental case, for example, management was unable to wrest labor concessions from its unions through negotiation. After purchasing Continental, Frank Lorenzo announced his desire to "provide all the frills of flying at discounted fares" (*Fortune*, January 9, 1984, 66–73). The only way to do this was by drastically reducing costs, and Lorenzo chose to focus on reducing labor costs. Shortly after purchasing Continental, Lorenzo imposed a 15 percent wage cut on non-union employees. He sought an additional $100 million in labor savings from unionized workers. After unsuccessfully attempting to achieve these cuts through bargaining with Continental's major unions, the firm unilaterally broke its labor contract by means of the bankruptcy process.

Through bankruptcy, Continental managed to achieve the labor cost reductions it had unsuccessfully sought outside the bankruptcy process. After emerging from Chapter 11, Continental reduced its cost per seat-mile from 8.5 cents to 6.3 cents by reducing its labor costs from 36 percent of total operating costs to 22 percent.

Texaco hoped to use Chapter 11 to frustrate Pennzoil's efforts to collect the $10.53 billion damage award granted it in connection with the takeover battle for the Getty Oil Company. The bankruptcy process was invoked by Texaco to improve its bargaining status with Pennzoil. All payments were "stayed" during Chapter 11, so Texaco did not have to pay the damages to Pennzoil until it emerged from bankruptcy. Pennzoil was forced into negotiating a reduction of the award.

Manville entered the Chapter 11 process to limit impending liability linked to injurious products. Manville faced the prospect of decades of lawsuits from customers, workers, and their families exposed to the firm's asbestos products. By invoking Chapter 11, Manville gained a collective compensation board system that bars punitive damages against the company. This promises to save the firm hundreds of millions of dollars as well as continued embarrassment by court testimony, which had been producing damaging evidence that Manville may have known about the danger of asbestos much earlier than it has publicly stated. Those injured or killed by asbestos will collect an average of only $30,000 to $50,000 per claim through the compensation board system (Delaney 1989a and 1989b).

Another way to perform this network surgery is by using a bankruptcy filing to shift *future* financial risk from one party to another. In the Manville bankruptcy, commercial creditors pushed for a Chapter 11 filing in hopes of fashioning a collective settlement to the asbestos crisis that reduced the risk of their outstanding loans to Manville. Just prior to Manville's Chapter 11 filing, creditors refused to lend additional money to the firm until the asbestos litigation was resolved.

After five years in Chapter 11, the firm emerged with a collective compensation scheme dependent on future profits. Commercial creditors received all of the money owed them, plus stocks and bonds in lieu of interest. Asbestos victims, however, must count on a fund dependent on the firm's profitability into the distant future. The fund has already run into financial trouble, facing a cash crisis that has delayed payments to asbestos victims (*NYT*, October 25, 1989, D1). In the Manville case, Chapter 11 became the vehicle for shifting financial risk from a more powerful organization (Morgan Guaranty) to a more vulnerable group (future asbestos victims).

Risk can also be shifted to parties that are completely external to the bankruptcy process. In the Manville case, financial risk was shifted to smaller asbestos manufacturers that did not declare bankruptcy. During Manville's five years under Chapter 11 protection, asbestos victims continued to sue other asbestos manufacturers, since they could not pursue Manville in court (recall that many asbestos cases were against numerous manufacturers, since the injured worker might have handled asbestos from several manufacturers). Lawyers, barred from pursuing Manville for five years, sued smaller asbestos manufacturers. In this way, the financial burden was shifted from Manville to other asbestos companies. Several of these smaller asbestos companies (e.g., Nicolet and Forty-Eight Insulations Inc.) have since been liquidated (*NYT*, April 2, 1989, c1).

Texaco's lenders used Chapter 11 as an opportunity to achieve a goal it had been seeking for years: forcing Texaco to use consortium financing. As part of its reorganization plan, Texaco agreed to several highly restrictive covenants that limited the banks' risk while constraining Texaco management's discretion. Thus, Texaco's lenders used bankruptcy as a strategic opportunity, not only to press for a settlement between Texaco and Pennzoil, but also to accomplish a goal, consortium financing with restrictive covenants, that had eluded them outside of bankruptcy.

Managers and large bank creditors dominated in these cases, and more vulnerable groups suffered owing to their lack of power over the debtor firm. A major form of this domination occurred through the shifting of financial risk described above. In the Manville case, for example, commercial creditors were able to get all of their money out of the firm on a fairly rapid schedule, while future asbestos victims will be dependent on a pool of money funded by a portion of Manville's profits over the next several decades. When the pool runs out of money, or should the firm end up back in bankruptcy, the asbestos victims will bear the brunt of the suffering. So this strategic bankruptcy shifted financial risk from a highly organized group of commercial creditors to a highly vulnerable group of future asbestos victims.

Similarly, in the Continental case, union workers bore the brunt of the reorganization. Again, bank creditors received all of their money back, with interest, on a fairly rapid schedule. In fact, Continental's original plan to repay commercial lenders was revised to increase the interest rate paid and reduce the length of the repayment period, both of which were in the lenders' interest. Union employees, however, lost their jobs or experienced a 50 percent cut in wages, lost seniority privileges, and were forced to accept changes in work rules. Management decided that the "cost of labor" was more amenable to reduction than "the cost of money" or the cost of equipment.

In the Texaco case, the only vulnerable group to shift burden or risk to was Pennzoil. The amount of the damage award was so large that Texaco's best option lay in negotiating a reduction of that award. Once Texaco decided to declare bankruptcy to frustrate its rival, Pennzoil's negotiating position was severely weakened and there was little it could do except bargain over reduction of the damage award. Bank creditors ended up getting all of their money repaid and obtained very restrictive loan covenants with the oil company. Texaco was forced to settle the case without finishing its appeal because commercial creditors and shareholders went around management to negotiate directly with Pennzoil.

Recognizing the strategic implications of the bankruptcy process suggests that we must continue to explore the various sources of power available to different parties in a bankruptcy proceeding. By this, I mean looking not only to formal rights and duties within the bankruptcy court but also to bases of power outside of the legal arena. For example, large commercial lenders have enormous leverage because the debtor company is likely to need their support, not only to survive the bankruptcy process, but also to gain passage of its reorganization plan and for future loans.

Will bankruptcy, then, always be chosen when firms face difficulty achieving their aims? The answer is, of course, no. There are significant costs attached to going bankrupt, though I have argued that those costs are declining. So organizations will not use the bankruptcy process cavalierly. But increasingly firms are looking to bankruptcy when they are thwarted in achieving organizational goals.

In some instances, firms can shift financial risk without using the bankruptcy process. In the case of Eagle-Pitcher (another asbestos manufacturer), the firm attempted to avoid bankruptcy while still achieving a court-mandated compensation board similar to Manville's. In an unprecedented legal decision, Judge Jack Weinstein tried to consolidate all of the asbestos cases against Eagle-Pitcher into a single suit and create a compensation system to replace individual lawsuits. If Weinstein had been successful, Eagle-Pitcher might have achieved exactly what Manville achieved without declaring bankruptcy. However, Eagle-Pitcher eventually declared bankruptcy and the legal effort collapsed.

WHY CHOOSE REORGANIZATION OVER LIQUIDATION?

I must propose what might seem like a very simple question: Why would commercial creditors prefer a bankruptcy reorganization over liquidation? Why not simply liquidate the firm, and get whatever money is possible out of the company and invest it elsewhere? The traditional legal and economic views hold that creditors and the court will push for reorganization when they estimate that assets are worth more kept together than sold off (Jackson 1986).

My theory of bankruptcy and the evidence in the cases discussed above lead me to a different answer. In strategic bankruptcies, there is great room for interpreting and defining the firm's liabilities, assets, and future value. In many cases, I think it is fair to say that no one knows what the firm is really worth. Cash, on the other hand, has a current, definitive value. Upon liquidation, the law clearly specifies what portion of the cash goes to each group. This is embodied in the bankruptcy principle of absolute priority. Each creditor resides on a certain priority level, and all creditors on the same level (at least in theory) get a pro rata share of what is owed them. In the Manville case, for example, unsecured bank creditors and future asbestos victims stood on the same priority level as "unsecured creditors." If Manville had been liquidated, each of these two sets of creditors would have been paid a portion of their claims against Manville, but surely less than 100 percent.

However, in a strategic bankruptcy reorganization (as opposed to liquidation), the parties begin to argue over "future assets" and "future liabilities," which are a lot less clear than cash, and are therefore subject to interpretation and manipulation. If bank creditors can successfully gain their definition of the future potential of the company and argue that future assets will be enough to cover *all* future liabilities as they come due, the banks can get all of their money repaid to them quickly. In the Manville case, for example, future estimated earnings were said to take care of future estimated asbestos liabilities. Bank creditors then got their risky investment out of Manville. If they decide to loan money to Manville in the future, they can charge higher interest rates or bargain for secured status. Future asbestos victims, however, are left with no one to collect from should the company not achieve the profits projected many decades into the future.

As I have shown, potential or future value is ripe for manipulation. If large lenders stand to take a loss upon the liquidation of the company, they can opt to precipitate a Chapter 11 reorganization in hopes of shifting financial risk or financial burden to less powerful and less organized groups. Thus, in strategic bankruptcies, which center on vague and arguable assets and debts, more powerful creditors might prefer Chapter 11 reorganization to either liquidation or continuation outside of bankruptcy. My analysis suggests that reorganization is not chosen when assets are worth more kept together than sold off, but rather when financial burden and future financial risk can be shifted to another party through bankruptcy.

IMPLICATIONS FOR COMPETING BANKRUPTCY THEORIES

I now return to competing theories of bankruptcy in light of the evidence from these cases. Strategic bankruptcies raise some important challenges to the dominant theories of the bankruptcy process.

Bankruptcy as the Relation of Assets to Debts

As discussed in chapter 2, most prediction models continue to treat bankruptcy as a technical relationship between asset and debt levels, as a state of affairs that a firm finds itself in, and as a last resort accepted by management when there is "no other choice." This view holds that managers at Manville, Texaco, and Continental chose Chapter 11 simply in response to economic forces.

This position misses how powerful institutions successfully shaped "official" financial data to benefit themselves at the expense of other groups. If financial data had been shaped differently, there might have been other choices available beside bankruptcy. The best evidence for this is that Manville itself argued for several years that since it could not estimate its liability for future asbestos-caused disease, it was not therefore an "official liability," and that the firm was thus not bankrupt, but quite healthy. Only when Manville's lenders helped shape the financial data in such a way as to include the liability was Manville deemed bankrupt. Manville's management and commercial creditors exercised control over when liabilities became "official." Asbestos victims lacked this power. For over a decade, they had unsuccessfully tried to get asbestos manufacturers to recognize their claims as "official."

This means that the power of various creditors helps determine whether a firm declares a strategic bankruptcy or whether it tries to solve its problems outside of bankruptcy. But the dominant market model of corporate bankruptcy continues to argue that ANY firm faced with the same balance-sheet data (similar liabilities and assets) and the same macroeconomic conditions (stage in the business cycle, national interest rates, etc.) might be expected to make the same choice (whether to declare bankruptcy or not)— assuming, of course, that firms act rationally.

I argue that knowing the balance-sheet figures and macroeconomic factors is not nearly enough to make this prediction. Strategic bankruptcies demonstrate that the nature of the firm's relationships with other organizations and the relative power of each organizational actor must also be assessed.

For example, consider Firm A, with liabilities of $500 million to asbestos victims, and Firm B, with an equal liability of $500 million, but to commercial lenders. Both creditors— asbestos victims and bank lenders—have equal standing under bankruptcy law regarding their claims against the debtor (they both are classified as "unsecured creditors"). Each debtor has the same amount of liabilities and assets. In this example, each debtor is in the same industry and stands in the larger market economy with similar national interest rates, at a similar stage in the business cycle, and so on. The market model would predict that both firms, acting rationally, will choose the same course of action (let's say, for the sake of this example, to declare bankruptcy).

I expect different decisions from the two firms. Firm A may decide that through Chapter 11 bankruptcy it can achieve a compensation system that will reduce its aggregate liability to the victims to only $400 million and spread payments over a long period. Firm B, on the other hand, may reckon that bankruptcy will not enable it to do the same with its liability to a commercial creditor. The reasoning is simple and is based on the power of the actor with which the debtor has the network tie (in this case the liability). Firm A gambles that if it can team up with its financial lenders, it might be able to get this plan through the bankruptcy court, while Firm B reasons that it stands much less of a chance of reducing a liability against a powerful group of commercial banks. Firm A might receive continued lending from its bankers, while Firm B is likely to be refused loans during prolonged bankruptcy proceedings, damaging Firm B even further. Factoring in all the negative costs of declaring bankruptcy (adverse publicity, stresses with suppliers and customers, etc.), it may be rational for Firm A to declare bankruptcy and for Firm B to steer clear of bankruptcy.

So in a scenario with the same balance-sheet data and the same macroeconomic factors, the rational decision for Firm A and Firm B differs. The deciding factor in this example is the nature of the tie with the creditor and the power of that creditor. If the creditor is a commercial bank, one course of action is deemed rational, while if the creditors are a mass of unknown future asbestos victims, the opposite course of action is rational. It is in this sense that the economic rationality of an organization's actions are embedded in social structure. The power of various actors with ties to the firm shape the very definition of what is economically rational. Thus, we cannot say that Firm A with x liabilities and y assets facing z market conditions will choose bankruptcy if it is a rational actor. We need also to know what type of liabilities the firm has. Are they concrete and indisputable or are they highly contestable? Who are the creditors and what are the sources of power available to them to shape the business crisis? What is the relationship between the firm and its various creditors?

Bankruptcy as a Mechanism
Ensuring Efficient Outcomes

A favorite metaphor used by the law-and-economics tradition to illustrate the efficiency and fairness of bankruptcy law is the "common pool" metaphor. "The single most fruitful way to think about bankruptcy is to see it as ameliorating a common pool problem. . . . Bankruptcy provides a way to override the creditors' pursuit of their own remedies and to make them work together," Thomas Jackson writes (1986, 16–17). The common pool is put forth as a metaphor for the bankruptcy situation and is used to illustrate how legal rules are designed to provide efficient outcomes, in which society is better off than it would be without bankruptcy. The common pool metaphor is almost always some variant of the following (see, e.g., Friedman 1971; Hardin 1968; Jackson 1986, 16–18): Let us suppose there are 1,000 fish in a pond worth $1 each when sold on the market. The owner of the pond could catch all 1,000 fish this year and make $1,000 by selling them. However, this leaves him with no fish (and therefore no income) for future years. If rational, the owner will catch only 500 fish this year and sell them for $500, but be able to catch another 500 next year, and so on forever.

Now let us suppose that the pond has, not one, but ten owners. The efficient solution for these ten owners is to act just like the single owner and catch 50 fish each (50 x 10 =

500). But a problem arises: how do we get the ten owners to behave like a single owner? In other words, how do we prevent one from grabbing all 1,000 fish and leaving none for the future? According to the metaphor, the ten owners would agree to a system that contains rules that influence, coerce, or force them to act as a single owner.

The bankruptcy system is said to do exactly this. Legal rules are supposed to prevent a single creditor from rushing in and grabbing all the assets, leaving none for the other creditors. Without bankruptcy rules, an "inefficient" solution might result from a single owner forcing the collapse of a productive company by pulling out a large chunk of its productive assets at the expense of other creditors, leaving them with nothing. It might be inefficient to pull out these assets, the argument goes, because if kept together they might provide more to the group of creditors. Some legal theorists, most notably Jackson (1986, 17) push the argument even further, though, by arguing that the owners would not only agree to a system of rules, but that the rules will be fair, because each owner would assent to such a system if asked in advance.

But what if the ten fishermen have unequal power? The strongest might *not* assent to this system, because he might do better without the intervention of legal rules by exercising his power (based on strength, money, information, and access to government officials or special legal knowledge). He might use this power to catch 75 fish, while a weaker fisherman gets only 25. A more powerful angler might even catch all the fish, exhausting the pond for the future, and move on to another pond, hoping to win again. Similarly, a weak angler might not assent to the rules either, knowing full well that they might continue the dominance of the more powerful fishermen.

Jackson counters (1986, 10–12) by arguing that all would assent to this arrangement if they were "bargaining behind a veil of ignorance." That is, if none of the fishermen *knew* who was strongest they would all agree to the rules because they provide the most efficient overall outcome. Despite the possibility of differential power, he concludes, the bankruptcy system is thus a "just bargain" (Rawls 1971).

Strategic bankruptcies illustrate some of the flaws in this simplistic metaphor. Let us first stick with the language of the metaphor itself. The metaphor assumes we know (1) how many fish there are in the pond, (2) what constitutes "the pond" (do we include the tributary that runs into the pond?), (3) how productive these little fish will be each year, and (4) the future value of the fish. In strategic bankruptcies, however, there are often great disputes over all of these issues. To put it in terms of a company: What is the company worth now? What constitutes the company? How productive is the company now? What will the company be worth in the future?

The evidence from strategic bankruptcies convincingly demonstrates that each of these questions has a variety of possible answers. If one of the ten owners of the pond is more powerful, he might force his answer to these questions on us. For example, he might argue:

> Based on my sophisticated estimating techniques and expert knowledge, there are actually 1,500 fish in this pond, not merely 1,000 as the other owners think, and I believe they will reproduce at a geometric rather than an arithmetic rate, so there will actually be 3,000 next year, 6,000 the following year, and 12,000 in the third year. Therefore, I can now safely and fairly take what is my due: 700 this year and 1,300 next year and I shall be done with my fishing in this pond. You (the less powerful fisherman) can take 200 each year for the next ten years and still get your rightful share.

Who has won here? If all works out according to the powerful fisherman's estimate of the number of fish and their reproductive rates, both may come out with what is owed them. But what if the powerful fisherman is wrong? What if there are really only 900 rather than 1,500 fish in the pond, and if they fail to reproduce at a geometric rate? Then he gets what is owed him in the first two years and the less powerful fisherman is left with very little. Not only does the powerful one win out, but a "less efficient" solution has been chosen. As in the cases I have analyzed, efficiency begins to fade and questions of power become crucial.

In this same way, financial burden and future financial risk in strategic bankruptcy can be shifted from more powerful creditors to less powerful ones. If the more powerful creditor can obtain definitions of current liabilities and assets and future liabilities and assets that favor it, the future risk of not getting paid can be shifted to less powerful groups. So it was in the Manville case. Bank creditors got their money out of the firm in rapid fashion, leaving future asbestos victims to count on the projected profitability of the firm into the next several decades.

There are severe weaknesses with the argument that all fishermen, or creditors, would assent to bankruptcy rules (see Carlson 1987). Sociologists have spent many years documenting the fact that people do not bargain behind a "veil of ignorance" in the real world. Not everyone has an equal chance of becoming a CEO or an asbestos factory worker. The asbestos installers might balk at the current bankruptcy rules (if we ever thought to ask them) after their experiences in the Manville case. Even more absurdly, according to this scheme, *future* asbestos victims (who do not yet know they have asbestosis) are said to have agreed to these bankruptcy rules as well!

Once we question the assumption that bankruptcy is a purely economic relationship between assets and debts, we must also question the larger theoretical issue of whether bankruptcy ensures an efficient national economy by neutrally weeding out inefficient firms. Clearly, bankruptcy is a key component of business exit. A number of diverse theorists from Schumpeter (1939) to Drucker (1974) to Jackson (1986) argue that the bankruptcy process allows efficient firms to reorganize and continue in business while providing for the liquidation of inefficient firms. This decision is supposedly based on whether the assets of the firm are worth more kept together or broken up and sold off through liquidation. The decision involves a series of valuations to determine what the company is currently worth, what it might be worth in the future, and what it would be worth if sold off.

As I have argued above, the valuation process can be manipulated. Estimating the current and future value of any company is a tricky process. The economic efficiency argument, however, rests on the assumption that the terms *liabilities, debts, assets,* and so on can be systematically, rigorously, and technically defined and thereby applied uniformly. To act as a neutral mechanism, bankruptcy requires that these definitions be applied uniformly. But if power is decisive in the very definition of these terms, then we cannot assume a priori that bankruptcy is a neutral, market-driven mechanism that ensures that weak firms are eliminated and strong firms survive. Evidence from the three cases analyzed here illustrates that these definitions can switch over time according to the power and interests of various institutional actors.

If seemingly apolitical, technical factors such as "debt" and "assets" are really open to manipulation by organizational actors, then we must address the issue of who has the power to influence them. We may find that there is more likelihood of powerful organizations (those that gain their definition of crucial terms) surviving the bankruptcy process intact than of more efficient firms (those producing at the least average cost) doing so.

In the cases analyzed in this book, it is unclear how each reorganization improved the *overall* efficiency of the general economy, one of the common themes in the literature on corporate bankruptcy. In fact, the court rarely addressed issues of efficiency. When they were addressed, they were based on organizationally constructed versions of "liability," "debt," "insolvent," and "bankrupt."

Perhaps the Texaco case provides the best example. There was little effort in the bankruptcy court to determine whether Texaco was an efficient company, or whether liquidating the company and selling off subsidiaries might improve the overall efficiency of the economy. It is not clear whether the overall efficiency of the economy would have been helped or hindered if Texaco had been broken up. Certainly, more evidence would have been needed to answer this question. But all parties accepted the notion that Texaco was in bankruptcy court solely to pressure a settlement with Pennzoil. Several judges in the case made a number of decisions that reflected their desire to keep the company together and avoid its liquidation at all costs. This notion of keeping the company intact is an extension of bankruptcy law's increasing stress on allowing firms to reorganize.

This goal, however, can clash with the purported role of bankruptcy as a weeding-out mechanism for inefficient firms. In *The Logic and Limits of Bankruptcy Law* (1986), Thomas Jackson argues that bankruptcy has a single "essence": debt collection, and that the law should not, and does not, have as one of its intended goals a "fresh start" for debtor corporations. Despite this scholarly attempt to ferret out a single, underlying role of the corporate bankruptcy process, it is clear that bankruptcy has fulfilled a variety of functions throughout history, as I demonstrated in chapter 1.

Despite Jackson's contention, my analysis suggests that legislators and judges quite often act as if a "fresh start" for companies is the primary goal of bankruptcy law. The goal of acting as an arbiter of efficiency and liquidating inefficient firms and the goal of trying to give a fresh start to troubled firms often clash. In bankruptcy cases, judges can use the language of efficiency or the language of fresh start to justify either keeping together or liquidating the firm. In the cases discussed, the spirit of the bankruptcy code and its stress on keeping companies intact had once again been extended.

Bankruptcy as a Reduction in Transaction Costs

A transaction-cost analysis suggests that bankruptcy provides an efficient solution to business crises, since it reduces the transaction costs associated with transferring the debt-or's assets to parties with valid claims against the company. Thus, for example, bankruptcy in the Manville case is said to be efficient because it reduces the transaction costs nec-essary to transfer assets from the debtor to the creditors (in-cluding asbestos victims).

Certain transaction costs were reduced in these cases. For example, lawyers' fees were probably reduced in the Man-ville case, since thousands of tort cases were not tried and instead will go before a compensation board. In this sense, a transaction-cost perspective is helpful in measuring the effi-ciency of a bankruptcy solution over a tort-based solution (i.e., numerous individual lawsuits). The more important criticism of this position, however, centers on the issue of fairness rather than efficiency. In the Manville case, for ex-ample, the reorganization plan does not simply allow more efficient collection of claims. As I have shown, the plan also shifts financial risk to the most vulnerable (and unorganized) group—future asbestos victims. Since Manville's liability to future victims is so difficult to estimate and extends far into the future, the financial risk of misestimation is shifted from commercial creditors to the future asbestos victims. Asbestos victims will only be able to collect if Manville can continue to fund the compensation fund for the next three decades. If Manville is unable to remain sufficiently profitable, or if the number of victims was underestimated, the future asbestos claimants will be unable to collect. This is exactly the prob-lem the compensation board ran into almost immediately. The compensation fund was faced with a far greater number of claims for more serious asbestos injuries than was esti-mated in the reorganization plan. The fund ran out of mon-ey, and asbestos victims have been forced to wait for a new infusion of cash. Commercial lenders, on the other hand, got their money out quickly. If they decide to loan money to Manville in the future, they can factor in the risk of Manville returning to bankruptcy court or liquidating by charging Manville higher interest rates, bargain for secured status (with a higher priority in court), or use restrictive loan covenants to constrain Manville's actions. This is an example of what I mean by the shifting of future financial risk to more vulnerable groups.

Additional evidence is necessary to ascertain whether asbestos victims will actually get as much out of the bankruptcy court settlement as they would through tort procedures. On the one hand, asbestos victims will save on lawyers' fees, and there is thus a reduction in transaction costs and the possibility that this will increase the total amount of assets available to victims. On the other hand, however, the bankruptcy settlement bars punitive damages, which clearly favors Manville at the expense of asbestos victims.

SOCIETAL IMPLICATIONS OF THE CHANGING
CONCEPTION OF THE "BANKRUPT"

These cases are not only a *result* of the historical process of widening the bankruptcy forum that I described in chapter 1. They are themselves *contributing* to this process. These large corporations spent a great deal of time and money convincing us that today Chapter 11 bankruptcy is different from going broke. Their message may be getting through to the general public. People will now line up and buy tickets on a "bankrupt" airline.

In a sense, the companies are right. Thanks to these and other cases, the bankruptcy arena is becoming something very different. Bankruptcy court is now a political arena where we are resolving such crucial social issues as the asbestos crisis, the IUD health crisis, the relationship between workers and owners, the sanctity of legally negotiated labor contracts and pension plans, and the rules of the corporate takeover game. We need to assess whether the bankruptcy arena is the proper place to make these decisions.

To use economic terms, we might say that the reduction in stigma and the widening of the bankruptcy forum has reduced the "cost" of going bankrupt, and, all else being equal, this will increase a firm's propensity to declare bankruptcy. If a firm can convince the public that it is in Chapter 11 for some limited, strategic reason and not because it is in real financial trouble, it will be more likely to choose bankruptcy, and its chances of surviving the bankruptcy process intact might increase. This desire to manage stigma explains why Manville took out full-page advertisements proclaiming "nothing is wrong with our businesses" the day after it had stated in its Chapter 11 filing that its asbestos liabilities would completely overwhelm its resources and that the firm was in truly dire straits. Manville surely realized that these advertisements would provide ammunition for asbestos groups arguing that the filing was a mere ploy to escape full liability and that the firm was in fact quite healthy. This risk, however, was apparently outweighed by the firm's desire to manage its corporate image and reassure lenders, suppliers, and customers that this was not a typical bankruptcy.

And these efforts at public relations are working. In the Continental bankruptcy, the airline persuaded enough customers that they could safely purchase tickets from Continental in the weeks following its bankruptcy filing. Certainly, these customers knew they were taking some risk with their money. There was a chance that these tickets would be worthless. However, the public's increasing willingness to see bankruptcy as a strategic move, rather than a kiss of death, allowed Continental to stay afloat during those first crucial weeks when its commercial lenders were deciding whether to support Lorenzo through the Chapter 11 process. Before long we may get to the point where travelers do not even blink at another airline bankruptcy.

The use of bankruptcy by our largest corporations and the changing perception of the bankrupt may thus encourage other firms to choose bankruptcy. This clearly does not mean a flood of new Chapter 11 cases from absolutely healthy firms; there are still real costs to declaring bankruptcy. But it does mean that a firm that wishes to alter a troublesome, contestable liability through bankruptcy will now be more likely to choose Chapter 11. Such a company can now find examples of other firms that have successfully managed their corporate images and survived the bankruptcy process. A business consultant who works with ailing firms has noticed this change: "Chapter 11 does not have the stigma it once had, when the mention of it could cause a client's face to redden and put tears in his eyes. Now the reaction is: I don't like it but my next-door neighbor did it. It can't be so bad" (*NYT*, March 25, 1984, business section, 8).

This decrease in the reluctance of firms to enter Chapter 11 can have both beneficial and harmful results for society. We may wish to reduce the reluctance of firms that are truly in financial trouble to enter a process designed to give the firm a "fresh start." If firms delay entering Chapter 11 because of stigma, viable companies may go broke because they waited too long to try to reorganize. At the same time, however, the reduction in stigma is encouraging more firms to use bankruptcy to avoid lawsuits; to decrease or eliminate damage awards for marketing injurious products, polluting, or other corporate misconduct; to abandon toxic waste sites; to break legally negotiated labor contracts; and to scrap pension and health insurance plans. With the aid of its largest creditors, a firm can shape its financial picture to gain access to Chapter 11. Once in the reorganization process, financial risk can be shifted away from more powerful institutional creditors and the corporation itself and onto the backs of more vulnerable groups. An increase in these cases thus promises to harm the more vulnerable and less organized groups in our society—the asbestos victims, workers, and individual shareholders who often seem to suffer as a result of strategic bankruptcy.

References

Alchian, Armen
  1953   "Biological Analogies in the Theory of the Firm: Comment." *American Economic Review* 43:600–603.
Aldrich, Howard
  1979   *Organizations and Environments.* Englewood Cliffs, N.J.: Prentice-Hall.
Alford, Robert, and Roger Friedland
  1985   *Powers of Theory.* Cambridge: Cambridge University Press.
Altman, Edward
  1968   "Financial Ratios, Discriminant Analysis and the Prediction of Corporation Bankruptcy." *Journal of Finance* 23:589–609.
  1971   *Corporate Bankruptcy in America.* Lexington, Mass.: Lexington Books.
  1973   "Predicting Railroad Bankruptcies in America." *Bell Journal of Economics* 4 (Spring): 184–211.
  1983   *Corporate Financial Distress: A Complete Guide to Predicting, Avoiding and Dealing with Bankruptcy.* New York: John Wiley & Sons.
American Law Institute
  1981   *Restatement of Contracts 2d.* St. Paul, Minn.: American Law Institute Publishers.
Ang, James, and Jess Chua
  1980   "Coalitions, the Me-First Rule, and the Liquidation Decision." *Bell Journal of Economics* 11:355–59.
Asbestos Litigation Group
  1983   "The Manville Bankruptcy: Using Chapter 11 as Escape Hatch." *Trial* 19 (February): 72–73.

Bacharach, Peter, and Morton Baratz
    1962   "The Two Faces of Power." *American Political Science Review* 56:947–52.
    1970   *Power and Poverty: Theory and Practice.* New York: Oxford University Press.
Bainbridge, J. S., Jr.
    1987   "Texaco's Last Stand." *American Bar Association Journal* 73 (August): 110–14.
Baird, Douglas
    1986   "The Uneasy Case for Corporate Bankruptcy." *Journal of Legal Studies* 15:127–47.
    1987a   "Loss Distribution, Forum Shopping and Bankruptcy: A Reply to Warren." *University of Chicago Law Review* 54:815–34.
    1987b   "A World without Bankruptcy." *Law and Contemporary Problems* 50:173–93.
Balin, Robert D.
    1983   "Kevin Steel and REA Express Revisited: When Is a Collective Bargaining Agreement Burdensome?" *Temple Law Quarterly* 56:252–83.
Baran, Paul A., and Paul M. Sweezy
    1966   *Monopoly Capital.* New York: Monthly Review Press.
Barrickman, Ray E.
    1979   *Business Failures: Causes, Remedies, Cures.* Washington, D.C.: University Press of America.
Baum, Daniel J., and Ned B. Stiles
    1965   *The Silent Partners: Institutional Investors and Corporate Control.* Syracuse, N.Y.: Syracuse University Press.
Bearden, James
    1982   "The Board of Directors in Large U.S. Corporations." Ph.D. diss., SUNY, Stony Brook, N.Y.
Beaver, William H.
    1968   "Market Prices, Financial Ratios and the Prediction of Failure." *Journal of Accounting Research* 6:179–92.
Berle, Adolf A., Jr.
    1954   *The 20th Century Capitalist Revolution.* New York: Harcourt, Brace & World.
Berle, Adolf A., Jr., and Gardiner C. Means
    1968   *The Modern Corporation and Private Property.* 1932. New York: Harcourt, Brace & World.

Berman, Jack
  1984   "Beshada v. Johns-Manville Products Corp.: The Func-
          tion of State of the Art Evidence in Strict Product Lia-
          bility." *American Journal of Law and Medicine* 10:
          93–114.
Bordewieck, Douglas, and Vern Countryman
  1983   "The Rejection of Collective Bargaining Agreements by
          Chapter 11 Debtors." *American Bankruptcy Law Journal*
          57:293–337.
Brodeur, Paul
  1985   "The Asbestos Industry on Trial." *New Yorker*
  a–d   Part 1. June 10:49–101.
          Part 2. June 17:45–111.
          Part 3. June 24:37–77.
          Part 4. July 1:36–80.
  1985e   *Outrageous Misconduct: The Asbestos Industry on Trial.*
          New York: Pantheon Books.
Brontë, Charlotte
  1975   *Shirley.* Edited by Andrew and Judith Hook. Harmonds-
          worth: Penguin Books.
Brown, Warren
  1988   "Surviving Creative Bankruptcy." *Washington Post,* No-
          vember 6, H1.
Browning, Graeme
  1984   "Using Bankruptcy to Reject Labor Contracts." *Ameri-
          can Bar Association Journal* 70 (February):60–63.
Burnham, James
  1941   *The Managerial Revolution.* New York: John Day.
Carlson, David
  1987   "Philosophy in Bankruptcy." *University of Michigan Law
          Review* 85:1341–89
Carlson, Elaine A.
  1987   "Mandatory Supersedeas Bond Requirements—A Denial
          of Due Process Rights?" *Baylor Law Review* 39(1):29–61.
Chen, Edward
  1984   "Asbestos Litigation Is a Growth Industry." *Atlantic*
          25(1):24–32.
Continental Airlines
  1988   *Fact Sheet.* Houston. September.
Copeland, R. M., P. E. Dascher, and D. L. Davison
  1980   *Financial Accounting.* New York: John Wiley & Sons.

Countryman, Vern
  1971   "A History of American Bankruptcy Law." *Commercial Law Journal* 81(June/July):226–32.
  1973   "Executory Contracts in Bankruptcy." Part 1. *Minnesota Law Review* 57:439–91.
  1976   "A History of American Bankruptcy Law." *Bankruptcy Law Journal* 81(6):226–32.
Croyle, James L.
  1978   "Industrial Accident Liability Policy of the Early Twentieth Century." *Journal of Legal Studies* 7:279–97.
Cyert, Richard M., and James G. March
  1956   "Organizational Factors in the Theory of Oligopoly." *Quarterly Journal of Economics* 70:44–64.
Day, Richard
  1975   "Adaptive Processes in Economic Theory." In *Adaptive Economic Models*, ed. R. Day and T. Groves, 1–38. New York: Academic Press.
Delaney, Kevin J.
  1985   "The Manville Corporation and Mass-Tort Bankruptcy: Legal Accommodation of Corporate Interest." Paper presented to the Eastern Sociological Society, Philadelphia, March.
  1989a "Power, Intercorporate Networks, and 'Strategic Bankruptcy.'" *Law & Society Review* 23(4):643–66.
  1989b "Control During Corporate Crisis: Asbestos and the Manville Bankruptcy." *Critical Sociology* 16(2–3):51–74. Reprinted in *International Journal of Health Care Services*, forthcoming, 1991.
Dewing, Arthur Stone
  1926   *The Financial Policy of Corporations.* New York: Ronald Press.
Dickens, Charles
  1974   *Dombey and Son.* Edited by Alan Horsman. Oxford: Clarendon Press.
  1979   *Little Dorrit.* Edited by H. P. Sucksmith. Oxford: Clarendon Press.
Drucker, Peter
  1974   *Management: Tasks, Responsibilities, Practices.* New York: Harper & Row.
Dun & Bradstreet
  yearly *Business Failure Record.* New York: Dun & Bradstreet Corporation.

Eckstein, Rick
  1990   "Discretion and Constraint: The Political Economy of the Shoreham Nuclear Plant." Ph.D. diss., SUNY, Stony Brook, N.Y.
Eliot, George
  1961   *The Mill on the Floss.* Edited by Gordon Haight. Boston: Houghton Mifflin.
Epidemiological Resources Inc. (ERI)
  1982   *Projections of Asbestos-Related Diseases, 1980–2009.* Final report, August 2, 1982. Introduced during *In re* Johns-Manville Corp., Bankr. Nos. 82B 11,656–11,676 (Bankr. S.D.N.Y., August 26, 1982).
Financial Accounting Standards Board (FASB)
  1975   *Opinion Number 5: Accounting for Contingencies.* Stamford, Conn.: Financial Accounting Foundation.
Fitch, Robert, and Mary Oppenheimer
  1970   "Who Rules the Corporations?" *Socialist Revolution*, part 1, 1(4):73–108; part 2, 1(5):61–114; part 3, 1(5): 33–94.
Fortgang, Chaim J., and Thomas Mayer
  1985   "Valuation in Bankruptcy." *UCLA Law Review* 32: 1061–1132.
Freiermuth, Edmond P.
  1989   *Turnaround: Avoid Bankruptcy and Revitalize Your Company.* Blue Ridge Summit, Pa.: Liberty House.
Friedman, Alan E.
  1971   "The Economics of the Common Pool: Property Rights in Exhaustible Resources." *UCLA Law Review* 18: 855–87.
Funkhouser, Robert, Kenneth Levine, Laurie McGhee, and David Mollon
  1986   "Texaco Inc. v. Pennzoil Co.: Some Thoughts on the Limits of Federal Court Power over State Court Proceedings." *Fordham Law Review* 54:767–824.
Galanter, Marc
  1974   "Why the Haves Come Out Ahead: Speculation on the Limits of Legal Change." *Law & Society Review* 9: 95–160.
Galbraith, John Kenneth
  1957   *Money: Whence It Came, Where It Went.* Boston: Houghton Mifflin.

Glasberg, Davita S.
  1981   "Corporate Power and Control: The Case of Leasco Corporation versus Chemical Bank." *Social Problems* 29(2): 104–16.
  1982   "Corporations in Crisis: Institutional Decision-making and the Role of Finance Capital." Ph.D. diss., SUNY, Stony Brook, N.Y.
  1985   "The Role of Finance Capital and the Social Construction of Crisis." *Insurgent Sociologist* 13:39–51.
  1989   *The Power of Collective Purse Strings: The Effect of Bank Hegemony on Corporations and the State.* Berkeley: University of California Press.

Glasberg, Davita, and Michael Schwartz
  1983   "Ownership and Control of Corporations." *Annual Review of Sociology* 9:311–32.

Goffinet, Christopher M.
  1987   "The $10.53 Billion Question—When Are Parties Bound? Pennzoil and the Use of Agreements in Principle in Mergers and Acquisitions." *Vanderbilt Law Review* 40: 1367–96.

Gordon, M. J.
  1971   "Towards a Theory of Financial Distress." *Journal of Finance* 26:347–56.

Gordon, Robert
  1945   *Business Leadership in the Large Corporation.* Washington, D.C.: Brookings Institution.

Granovetter, Mark
  1985   "Economic Action and Social Structure: The Problem of Embeddedness." *American Journal of Sociology* 91(3):481–510.

Hannan, Michael, and John Freeman
  1977   "The Population Ecology of Organizations." *American Journal of Sociology* 82:924–64.

Hardin, Garrett
  1968   "The Tragedy of the Commons." *Science* 162 (December 13):1243–48.

Haydel, D'Anne
  1984   "Bildisco: Are Some Creditors More Equal than Others?" *South Carolina Law Review* 35:573–615.

Herman, Edward S.
  1973   "Do Bankers Control Corporations?" *Monthly Review* 25:12–29.

1979   "Kotz on Banker Control." *Monthly Review* 31:46–57.
1981   *Corporate Control, Corporate Power.* Cambridge: Cambridge University Press.
Hermann, Donald H. J., and David M. Neff
1985   "Rush to Judgment: Congressional Response to Judicial Recognition of Collective Bargaining Agreements under Chapter 11 of the Bankruptcy Code." *Arizona Law Review* 27:617–52.
Hirschman, Albert
1970   *Exit, Voice and Loyalty: Responses to Decline in Firms, Organizations and States.* Cambridge, Mass.: Harvard University Press.
Hutchinson, Ruth, Arthur Hutchinson, and Mabel Newcomer
1938   "Studies in Business Mortality." *American Economic Review* 28:497–514.
Jackson, Thomas H.
1982   "Bankruptcy, Non-Bankruptcy Entitlements, and the Creditors' Bargain." *Yale Law Journal* 91:857–907.
1986   *The Logic and Limits of Bankruptcy Law.* Cambridge, Mass.: Harvard University Press.
Johnson, Craig
1970   "Ratio Analysis and the Prediction of Firm Failure." *Journal of Finance* 25:1166–72.
Johnson, William G., and Edward Heler
1984   "Compensation for Death from Asbestos." *Industrial and Labor Relations Review* 37:529–40.
Kammerschen, David R.
1968   "The Influence of Ownership and Control on Profit Rates." *American Economic Review* 58(3): 432–47.
Kaysen, Carl
1957   "The Social Significance of the Modern Corporation." *American Economic Review* 47:311–19.
Kennedy, Frank R.
1980   "A Brief History of the Bankruptcy Reform Act." *North Carolina Law Review* 58(4): 667–80.
King, Lawrence P.
1973   "The Business Reorganization Chapter of the Proposed Bankruptcy Code—Or Whatever Happened to Chapters X, XI and XII?" *Commercial Law Journal* 78(12):429–36.
Leinsdorf, David, and Donald Etra
1973   *Citibank.* New York: Grossman.

Lukes, Steven
1974   *Power: A Radical View.* London: Macmillan.
McDaniel, Morey W.
1983   "Are Negative Pledge Clauses in Public Debt Issue Obsolete?" *Business Lawyer* 38: 867–81.
Manville Facts
1984   Denver: Corporate Relations Department, Manville Corporation.
March, James, and Herbert Simon
1958   *Organizations.* New York: John Wiley & Sons.
Marris, Robin
1964   *The Economic Theory of Managerial Capitalism.* London: Macmillan.
Marsh, Gene A., and David C. Cheng
1985   "The Impact of the Bankruptcy Reform Act on Business Bankruptcy Filings." *Alabama Law Review* 36 (Winter): 515–47.
Mayer, Martin
1974   *The Bankers.* New York: Weybright & Talley.
Mayhew, Leon H.
1975   "Institutions of Representation: Civil Justice and the Public." *Law & Society Review* 9:401–29.
Merrick, Richard L.
1986   "The Bankruptcy Dynamics of Collective Bargaining Agreements." *John Marshall Law Review* 19:301–63.
Meyer, Paul, and Howard Pifer
1970   "Prediction of Bank Failures." *Journal of Finance* 25:853–68.
Miller, Harvey R.
1984   "Chapter 11 of the Bankruptcy Act and Collective Bargaining Agreements." *Fordham Law Review* 52:1120–33.
Mintz, Beth, and Michael Schwartz
1981   "Interlocking Directorates and Interest Group Formation." *American Sociological Review* 46(6):851–69.
1985   *The Power Structure of American Business.* Chicago: University of Chicago Press.
Mizruchi, Mark
1982   *The Structure of the American Intercorporate Network, 1904–1974.* Beverly Hills, Calif.: Sage.
Mizruchi, Mark, and Michael Schwartz, eds.
1987   *Intercorporate Relations.* New York: Cambridge University Press.

Moller, Arthur B., and David B. Foltz, Jr.
  1980 "Chapter 11 of the 1978 Bankruptcy Code." *North Carolina Law Review* 58(5):881–924.
Moody's Industrial Manual
  yearly Moody's Investor Services. New York.
Murphy, Michael E.
  1986 *The Airline That Pride Almost Bought: The Struggle to Take Over Continental Airlines.* New York: F. Watts.
Neilson, Leonard E.
  1984 "America's Airlines Discover Chapter 11: Is It Reorganization or Union-busting?" *Journal of Contemporary Law* 11:365–87.
Nelson, Nancy L.
  1972 "Asbestos: Airborne Danger." *Safety Standards* 21(3): 2–7.
Nelson, Philip B.
  1981 *Corporations in Crisis: Behavioral Observations in Bankruptcy.* New York: Praeger.
Palmer, Donald, Roger Friedland, P. Devereaux Jennings, and Melanie E. Powers
  1987 "The Economics and Politics of Structure: The Multidivisional Form." *Administrative Science Quarterly* 32: 25–48.
Perrow, Charles
  1981 "Markets, Hierarchy and Hegemony." In *Perspectives on Organizational Design and Behavior,* ed. Andrew Van de Ven and William Joyce, 371–86. New York: John Wiley & Sons.
  1986 *Organizations: A Critical Essay.* 3d ed. New York: Random House.
Petzinger, Thomas
  1987 *Oil and Honor: The Texaco-Pennzoil Wars.* New York: Putnam.
Pfeffer, Jeffrey
  1972a "Size and Composition of Corporate Boards of Directors: The Organization and Its Environment." *Administrative Science Quarterly* 17:218–28.
  1972b "Merger as Response to Organizational Interdependence." *Administrative Science Quarterly* 17:382–94.
Pfeffer, Jeffrey, and Gerald Salancik
  1978 *The External Control of Organizations: A Resource Dependence Perspective.* New York: Harper & Row.

Platt, Harlan
  1985   *Why Companies Fail: Strategies for Detecting, Avoiding and Profiting from Bankruptcy.* Lexington, Mass.: Lexington Books.
Posner, Richard A.
  1972   *Economic Analysis of Law.* Boston: Little, Brown.
Ratcliffe, Richard E.
  1979–   "Capitalist Class Structure and the Decline of the Older
  80   Industrial Cities." *Insurgent Sociologist* 9:60–74.
Ratcliffe, Richard E., K. Oehler, and M. Gallops
  1979   "Networks of Financial Power: An Analysis of the Impact of the Internal Structure of the Capitalist Class on the Lending Behavior of Banks." Paper presented to the American Sociological Association, Boston.
  1980   "Banks and the Command of Capital Flows: An Analysis of Capitalist Class Structure and Mortgage Disinvestment in a Metropolitan Area." In *Classes, Conflict and the State*, ed. M. Zeitlin, 107–32. Cambridge, Mass.: Winthrop.
Ratcliffe, Richard E., M. E. Gallagher, and K. S. Ratcliffe
  1979   "The Civic Involvement of Business Leaders: An Analysis of the Influence of Economic Power and Social Prominence in the Command of Civil Policy Positions." *Social Problems* 26:298–313.
Rawls, John
  1971   *A Theory of Justice.* Cambridge, Mass.: Harvard University Press, Belknap Press.
Roberts, Gary M.
  1987   "Bankruptcy and the Union's Bargain: Equitable Treatment of Collective Bargaining Agreements." *Stanford Law Review* 39:1015–56.
Rockefeller, David
  1964   *Creative Management in Banking.* New York: McGraw-Hill.
Roe, Mark
  1984   "Bankruptcy and Mass Tort." *Columbia Law Review* 84:846–922.
Rome, Donald Lee
  1979   "The New Bankruptcy Act and the Commercial Lender." *Banking Law Journal* 96:389–417.

Rosenberg, Robert J.
1975 "Corporate Rehabilitation under the Bankruptcy Act of 1973: Are Reports of the Demise of Chapter XI Greatly Exaggerated?" *North Carolina Law Review* 53(6): 1149–96.

Royce, Edward
1985 "The Origins of Southern Sharecropping: Explaining Social Change." *Current Perspectives in Social Theory* 6:279–99.
1989 *Social Change and the Constriction of Possibilities.* Philadelphia: Temple University Press.

Sadd, Victor, and Robert T. Williams
1932 *Causes of Commercial Bankruptcies.* Washington, D.C.: Government Printing Office.

Sampson, Anthony
1984 *Empires of the Sky: The Politics, Contests and Cartels of World Airlines.* London: Hodder & Stoughton.

Schumpeter, Joseph A.
1939 *Business Cycles.* Vols. 1 and 2. New York: McGraw-Hill.
1950 *Capitalism, Socialism and Democracy.* 1942. New York: Harper & Row.

Selikoff, Irving
1982 "Asbestos-associated Disease." Reprinted in *Asbestos Litigation*, ed. W. Alcorn. New York; Harcourt Brace Jovanovich.

Selznick, Philip
1966 *TVA and the Grass Roots.* New York: Harper Torchbooks.

Serling, Robert J.
1974 *Maverick: The Story of Robert Six and Continental Airlines.* Garden City, N.Y.: Doubleday.
1980 *From the Captain to the Colonel: An Informal Analysis of Eastern Airlines.* New York: Dial Press.
1982 *The Jet Age.* Alexandria, Va.: Time-Life Books.

Shoven, James, and Jeremy Bulow
1978 "The Bankruptcy Decision." *Bell Journal of Economics* 9:437–56.

Simon, Herbert A.
1976 *Administrative Behavior.* 1947. 3d ed. New York: Free Press.

Stanley, David T., and Marjorie Girth
1971 *Bankruptcy: Problem, Process, Reform.* Washington, D.C.: Brookings Institution.

Starbuck, William H.
   1965   "Organizational Growth and Development." In *Handbook of Organizations*, ed. J. G. March, 451–533. Chicago: Rand McNally.
Stein, Gary
   1986   "Expanding the Due Process Rights of Indigent Litigants: Will Texaco Trickle Down?" *New York University Law Review* 61:463–505.
Sullivan, Teresa, Elizabeth Warren, and Jay Lawrence Westbrook
   1987   "The Use of Empirical Data in Formulating Bankruptcy Policy." *Law and Contemporary Problems* 50:195–235.
Thackeray, William Makepeace
   1963   *Vanity Fair: A Novel without a Hero*. Edited by Geoffrey and Kathleen Tillotson. Boston: Houghton Mifflin.
Thompson, James D.
   1967   *Organizations in Action*. New York: McGraw-Hill.
Thompson, James D., and William J. McEwen
   1958   "Organizational Goals and Environment: Goal Setting as an Interactive Process." *American Sociological Review* 23(1):23–31.
Tremain, Israel
   1927   "Escaping the Creditor in the Middle Ages." *Law Quarterly Review* 43:230–37.
   1938   "Acts of Bankruptcy: A Medieval Concept in Modern Bankruptcy Law." *Harvard Law Review* 52:189–215.
Trollope, Anthony
   1941   *The Way We Live Now*. London: Oxford University Press.
Turkel, Gerald
   1982   "Situated Corporatist Legitimacy: The 1980 Chrysler Loan Guarantee." *Research in Law, Deviance and Social Control* 4:165–89.
U.S. Code Congressional and Administrative News
   1978a   *Senate Report on the Bankruptcy Reform Act*, pp. 5787–5962. Washington, D.C.: Government Printing Office.
   1978b   *House Report on the Bankruptcy Reform Act*, pp. 5963–6435. Washington, D.C.: Government Printing Office.
U.S. House of Representatives. Committee on Education and Labor. Subcommittee on Labor Standards. 97th Cong., 2d sess.
   1982   *Oversight Hearings on the Effect of the Manville and UNR Bankruptcies on Compensation of Asbestos Victims*.

U.S. Senate. Committee on the Judiciary. Subcommittee on the Courts. 97th Cong., 2d sess.
1982   *The Manville Bankruptcy and the Northern Pipeline Decision.*

Useem, Michael
1980   "Corporations and Corporate Elite." *Annual Review of Sociology* 6:41–77.

Vartan, Vartanig G.
1986   "Funds Focus: Bankruptcies." *New York Times,* September 10, 1986, D8.

Vermeulen, James E., and Daniel M. Berman
1982   "Asbestos Companies under Fire." *Business and Society Review* 42:21–25.

Vian, John
1986   "The Rejection of Collective Bargaining Agreements since the 1984 Amendments: The Case Law under New Bankruptcy Code Section 1113." *Commercial Law Journal* 91:252–66.

Warren, Charles
1935   *Bankruptcy in United States History.* Cambridge, Mass.: Harvard University Press.

Warren, Elizabeth
1987   "Bankruptcy Policy." *University of Chicago Law Review* 54:775–814.

Weiss, Barbara
1986   *The Hell of the English: Bankruptcy and the Victorian Novel.* London: Associated University Presses.

Weistart, John C.
1977   "The Costs of Bankruptcy." *Law and Contemporary Problems* 41:107–22.

Weston, J. Fred
1977   "Some Economic Fundamentals for an Analysis of Bankruptcy." *Law and Contemporary Problems* 41:47–65.

White, James J.
1984   "The Bildisco Case and the Congressional Response." *Wayne Law Review* 30:1169–1204.

White, Michelle J.
1989   "The Corporate Bankruptcy Decision." *Journal of Economic Perspectives* 3:129–51.

Williamson, Oliver E.
1975   *Markets and Hierarchies: Analysis and Antitrust Implications.* New York: Free Press.

1985   *The Economic Institutions of Capitalism: Firms, Markets, Relational Contracting.* New York: Free Press.

Zeitlin, Maurice
1974   "Corporate Ownership and Control: The Large Corporation and the Capitalist Class." *American Journal of Sociology* 79(5):1073–1119.

Zemans, Frances Kahn
1982   "Framework for Analysis of Legal Mobilization: Decision-making Model." *American Bar Foundation Research Journal* 4:989–1071.

1983   "Legal Mobilization: The Neglected Role of the Law in the Political System." *American Political Science Review* 77(3):690–703.

Zurofsky, Bennett D.
1987   "Repudiation of Collective Bargaining Agreements in Bankruptcy—A Practical History and Guide for Union Representatives." *Labor Lawyer* 3:809–16.

Index

"Act against Such Persons as Do Make Bankrupt," 14
Adams, Richard, 94
AFL-CIO, 112
Airline Deregulation Act of 1978, 85–86
Airline fares, 86–87, 89, 93, 102, 103–4, 119
Airline industry, deregulation of, 84–88, 117–18
Air Line Pilots Association, 100
Alan Wood test, 108–9
American Federation of Labor (AFL), 112
Asbestos: history of health problems with, 61, 75; uses of, 60; victims of, 1, 54, 72, 73, 148. *See also* Eagle-Pitcher; Manville Corporation
Asbestos Workers Recovery Act (AWRA), 65–66
Assets: future, 167, 177–78; shifting of, 97–98, 99, 161, 163, 164–65; term subject to interpretation, 4, 122, 162, 185
Automated reservation system, 117–18

Babbitt (judge), 167
Balance sheet: organizational construction of, 41, 163–64
Balance sheet insolvency, 29
"Balancing of the equities," 108
Bank-control theory, 52
Banking Law Journal, 32
Banking syndicates, 137, 153
Bank of America, 143
Bankruptcy, 3, 7, 26, 176; business, 6–7, 11–12, 26, 161–62; defined and derivation of, 11, 57–58; efficiency of current process questioned, 117–18, 124, 159, 181–86; historic sanctions against, 12, 14, 15–16, 19–20; increase in filings of, 23, 26; involuntary, 68, 68n; political arena of, 3, 23, 41, 59, 80–81, 125, 162, 179–81, 184, 188; popular conceptions of, 16–17, 37–38, 38n, 41–42, 58; reduction of stigma attached to, 19–20, 21–22, 34, 101, 146–47, 156, 189; social goals pertaining to, 5–6, 35, 124; *See also* Bankruptcy, theories of; Bankruptcy law;

Bankruptcy (*continued*)
Bankruptcy process; Claim to
bankruptcy; Continental
bankruptcy; Manville
bankruptcy; Organizational
construction theory; Strategic
bankruptcy; Texaco
bankruptcy
Bankruptcy, theories of, 36, 37;
academic, 4; economic/
market, 39–42, 55–56, 74,
162, 169, 178–88; law-and-
economics, 42–47. *See also*
Finance hegemony;
Managerialism;
Organizational construction
theory; Resource dependency
school
Bankruptcy Act of 1841, 20, 106
Bankruptcy Act of 1867, 21–22
Bankruptcy Act of 1869
(British), 105
Bankruptcy Act of 1898, 16n,
21–22, 70, 122
Bankruptcy court, 30–31, 45–
46, 118, 149; acted to protect
Texaco, 139–41, 145
Bankruptcy law: changes in,
leading to current, 27–34, 81,
122–23; and collective
bargaining agreements, 105–
12, 115–16, 118–19, 122;
"cram down" provision of,
73; extended to businesses,
20–21; and institution of
voluntary bankruptcy, 20;
reacting to economic
upheavals, 18–20, 22–23, 58;
roots of, 12–17, 19–20;
specialists in, 33–34, 97; use
vs. intent of, 45–46, 70–71,

144–46, 160–61. *See also by
individual law*
Bankruptcy process, 39, 95–
105; efficiency of questioned,
185–86
Bankruptcy Reform Act of
1978, 25–34, 70, 105, 170
Bankrupt unit: defining the, 98,
120–21, 125, 145, 164;
shifting assets from, 164–65
Banks. *See* Creditors,
commercial
Baxter, Larry, 94
Berle, Adolf A., Jr., 48, 49
"Big Four" (airlines), 84
"Big Three" (auto
manufacturers), 55
Bildisco case, 107, 109–11, 123;
reaction to, 112
Borman, Frank, 104
Bottom line: organizational
construction of, 162–67
Braniff Airways, 86, 121
Brescia, Al, 86
Brieant, Charles, 141, 142, 157
Brontë, Charlotte, 15
Brookings Institution study,
25–26, 38
Brotherhood of Railway,
Airline, and Steamship Clerks
v. REA Express, 108
Burnham, James, 48
Burr, Donald, 86
Business bankruptcy, 6–7, 11–
12, 26; continuum of, 161–62
"Business judgment" standard,
111, 123

Capitalization rate, 166
Carney, Robert, 88–89

Carter, James E., Jr. (Jimmy), 28, 85
Cash. *See* Money
Cash-flow crisis, 121–22
Casseb, Solomon, 135, 137
Chandler Act of 1938, 22, 23–25
Chapter 11, 1, 11, 24–25, 30; challenged by SEC, 25; use of by large corporations, 27. *See also* Bankruptcy, business; Bankruptcy process; Strategic bankruptcy
Chapter X, 23, 27; consolidated into Chapter XI, 30
Chapter XII, 30
Chase Manhattan Bank, 89, 92, 113–14, 143
Civil Aeronautics Board (CAB), 84, 85, 89, 90, 117
Claim to bankruptcy: Continental's construction of, 120–21; definition of, 29; Manville's construction of, 74–81
Collateral, 121–22
Collective bargaining agreements, 9, 96, 108–11, 116; as executory contract, 105–9
Commission on the Bankruptcy Laws of the United States, 25, 28
"Common pool" metaphor, 181–84
Congress of Industrial Organizations (CIO), 112
Consortium financing, 137, 153, 174–75
Continental Airlines, 1–2, 3, 82–83; cost structure of, 114 table, 120; dispute with unions, 105–12, 115–16, 118–19, 122; early relationship with employees, 83–84; fought takeover by Texas International, 90–93; reorganization plans of, 115–16, 116 table. *See also* Continental bankruptcy
Continental bankruptcy: achieved reduction in labor costs, 172–73; commercial creditors' role in, 113–15, 119, 170, 171–72; filing and process of, 95–105; management actions in, 91–92, 121; response of competitors to, 103–5, 120. *See also* Continental Airlines
Contract: enforceability of, 130–32, 156; executory, 105–6
Coopers & Lybrand, 77
Corporate bankruptcy. *See* Business bankruptcy; Management; Strategic bankruptcy
Countryman, Vern, 100
Covenants, restrictive, 153, 175
"Cram down" provision, 73
Crandall, Robert, 86
Creditors, commercial: acting as a group, 181–82; Chase Manhattan Bank, 89, 92, 113–14, 143; concern over increase in bankruptcies, 26; Morgan Guaranty, 71, 169, 171; power of, 52–53, 56, 168–72, 177–79; role of in Continental case, 103, 113–15, 119, 170, 171–72; role of in Manville case, 67–69, 71–

Creditors (*continued*)
72, 78, 124, 168–69; role of in
Texaco bankruptcy, 147–48,
153, 154–55, 169–70, 170–71,
174–75
Creditors' committee, 27, 31–
33, 151–52
Cullinan, Joseph, 126

Dalkon Shield, 3, 9
Damages. *See* Liabilities, court-
imposed
DeArmond, David, 21
Debtor rehabilitation, 22, 186
Debts: predicting future, 167;
term subject to
interpretation, 7, 185. *See
also* Liabilities
Depression, Great, 22, 23
Deregulation, of airline
industry, 84–88, 117–18
Dickens, Charles, 15
Dombey and Son (Dickens), 15
Dun & Bradstreet: on business
failures, 37, 38

Eagle-Pitcher, case of, 176
Eastern Air Lines, 3, 86, 104
Economic models of
bankruptcy, 39–42, 55–56,
74, 162, 169, 178–88
Economic rationality, 55–58
Eliot, George, 15
Empires of the Sky (Sampson),
84
Employee Stock Ownership
Plan (ESOP), 92–93
Equipment costs, 118
Equities test, 108, 110, 111
Equity insolvency, 29–30, 122
Exclusivity plan, 151

Fares, airline, 86–87, 89, 93,
102, 103–4, 119
Feldman, Alvin, 90–91
Ferris, Richard, 104
Fessenden, William, 23
Finance hegemony, 52–53
Financial Accounting Standards
Board (FASB), 66–67, 75
Fourteenth Amendment, 138,
139
Freeman, Audrey, 112
"Fresh start," 22, 186
Friedman, David, 150
Fuel costs, 118

Getty, Gordon, 128–29
Getty, J. Paul, 128
Getty, Sarah, trust, 128
Getty Oil Company: battle over
acquisition of, 128–30, 131,
149, 157
Girth, Marjorie, 26
Gold, Lawrence, 112
Goldman Sachs, 128
Government: actions of in
Manville, 64–66, 77. *See also*
Bankruptcy court;
Bankruptcy law
Granovetter, Mark, 56
"Great Deregulator, The," 85

Haldeman, Robert, 85
Hirschman, Albert, 55
Holmes à Court, Robert, 150
Hulce, J. T., 71

Icahn, Carl, 150–52
"Imminent collapse" standard,
110, 123
Income, predicting future, 166–
67

Indigents, rights of, 138, 141
Insolvency, 17, 29, 98
Insurance companies, 62–64, 76
Intercorporate power, 49
Interlocks, corporate, 78, 78n
International Association of
  Machinists (IAM), 84, 94–95,
  100
Intrauterine device (IUD), 3
Involuntary bankruptcy, 68,
  68n

Jackson, Thomas H., 181–82
Jamail, Joe, 132
Johns-Manville. *See* Manville
  Corporation
Johnson, Lyndon B., 84
Judges, role of, 30–31, 45–46

Kahn, Arthur, 90
"Keeping house," 13, 14
Kennedy, Frank, 28
Kerr, Baine, 144
Kevin Steel Products case, 107,
  108, 109
Kidder, Peabody, 91
Kinnear, James, 152

Labor. *See* Bildisco case;
  Collective bargaining
  agreements; Labor costs;
  Unions
Labor costs, 94–95; compared
  with other costs, 118;
  reduced by Continental
  bankruptcy, 99, 100, 113,
  116–24, 172–73. *See also*
  Unions
Labor law: clash with
  bankruptcy law, 105–12,
  115–16, 118–19, 122

"Law of Agreements in
  Principle with a Formal
  Contract Contemplated, The,"
  131
Legal strategies, 167–68
Lenders. *See* Creditors,
  commercial
Liabilities, 1; selective
  recording of, 161, 163; term
  subject to interpretation, 4, 7,
  185. *See also* Debts;
  Liabilities, court-imposed
Liabilities, court-imposed:
  reduced by Manville
  bankruptcy, 3, 173–74, 178;
  in Texaco case, 132–37, 141,
  142, 157, 158–59. *See also*
  Liabilities
Liedtke, Hugh, 132, 144, 152
Linguistic strategies, 146–47,
  167. *See also* Public relations
  efforts
Liquidation, 4; compared to
  reorganization, 177–78;
  Texaco protected from, 139–
  41
Little Dorrit (Dickens), 15
Lorenzo Carney Company. *See*
  Lorenzo, Frank; Texas
  International Airlines
Lorenzo, Frank, 2, 3, 88–96
  passim, 116, 117
Lukes, Steven, 53, 54

Macroeconomic theories of
  bankruptcy, 40–41, 74
Maldutis, Julius, 104
Management, 165; actions of in
  Continental case, 91–92, 121;
  actions of in Manville case,

Management (*continued*)
69–70; benefits to in Texaco
case, 154–55
Managerialism, 48–50
Manville bankruptcy: actions of
board of directors, 69–70;
auditors' role in, 66–67, 77;
commercial creditors' role in,
78, 124, 168–69, 171, 173–74;
debt rating lowered, 67–69;
government refusal to
intervene in, 64–66, 77;
impending liability reduced
in, 173–74; insurers'
withdrawal from, 62–64, 76;
Morgan Guaranty's role in,
71, 169, 171; reorganization
plan for, 71–74, 80; use of
bankruptcy code in, 70–71.
See also Asbestos; Liabilities;
Manville Corporation
Manville Corporation, 1, 60–62;
litigation against, 61–62. *See
also* Manville bankruptcy
Market model, 6–7, 39–42, 124
Means, Gardiner C., 48
"Merchants That Run Away
with Other Men's Goods," 14
Microeconomic models of
bankruptcy, 39
Miller, Harvey, 22
Mill on the Floss, The (Eliot), 15
Mintz, Beth, 76
*Modern Corporation and Private
Property, The* (Berle and
Means), 48
Money: Continental's loss of,
96–97, 121–22; cost of, 99,
118; distributed in
liquidation, 177

Moody's Investor Services, 62,
67, 153
Morgan Guaranty, 71, 169, 171
Musselman, Frank, 113–14

National Labor Relations
Board (NLRB), 110, 111
Network relationships, 80
Nixon, Richard M., 85
Non-union employees, 95

Oligopoly, 55, 84, 85, 86–87
Organizational construction
theory, 39, 47–48, 53–55,
162–68; applied to
Continental case, 117, 124–
25; applied to Manville case,
74–81; applied to Texaco
case, 144–48, 154–59; and
intercorporate relations, 49,
50–51, 168–72; and social
relations, 56–57
Organization of Petroleum
Exporting Countries (OPEC),
127
Organized labor. *See* Unions

Parker, G. Earl, 64, 68
Parliament (British), 16
Pennzoil: attempt by to acquire
Getty Oil, 129; and conflict
with Texaco, 130–34; court-
awarded damages to, 132–34,
135; and negotiated
settlement with Texaco, 148,
152–53; trial strategy of,
131–32, 156
Pension rights, 107
People Express, 86, 104
Personal bankruptcy, 26

Power: dimensions of, 53–55.
See also Bankruptcy: political
arena of; Creditors,
commercial: power of
Public relations efforts, 4; of
Continental, 96, 189; of
Manville, 189; of Pennzoil,
131–32; of Texaco, 127, 146–
47
Pundsack, Frederick, 75
Putnam, Howard, 86

Rationality, economic, 55–58
Reconstruction Finance
Corporation, 23
Rehnquist, William, 110
Rental agreements, 105
Reorganization, 23, 43; chosen
over liquidation and tort
litigation, 79, 177–78;
creditors' participation in,
32; management control
during, 30. *See also*
Reorganization plans
Reorganization plans: in
Continental bankruptcy, 115–
16, 116 table; in Manville
bankruptcy, 71–74, 80; in
Texaco bankruptcy, 149–50,
151, 152–54
Reorganized entity, 165
Resource dependency school,
50–51
Resources: allocation of scarce,
5. *See also* "Common pool"
metaphor
Restricted assets, 122
Risk, shifting of future, 173–74,
178
Roberts, T. Glover, 115

Robins, A. H., 3, 33, 81
Roosevelt, Franklin D., 84
Rosenberg, Robert J., 32, 165–
66
Royce, Edward, 53

Salinger, Pierre, 84
Salomon Brothers, 104
Sampson, Anthony, 84
"Sanctuary," 13, 14
Sarah Getty trust, 128
Schroeder, John, 71
Schwartz, Michael, 76
Schwartzberg, Howard, 150,
152, 158
Securities and Exchange
Commission (SEC), 24, 25, 76,
135, 149
Seniority rights, 107
Shirley (Brontë), 15
Simon, Bruce, 112
Six, Robert, 82, 90
Skadden, Arps, 33
Smith, William, 104
Smith Barney, Harris Upham &
Co., 91
Solvency, 140
Southwest Airlines, 89
Standard & Poor's, 153
Stanley, David, 26
Stockholders: in Manville case,
72, 73
Strategic bankruptcy: key
elements of, 16; legal changes
enabling, 33, 34; to meet
corporate goals, 4, 5, 79, 94,
124, 146, 147, 148, 154–59,
172–76; and power, 53–55;
social costs of, 179, 188–90.
See also Bankruptcy: political

Strategic bankruptcy (*continued*)
  arena of; Organizational
  construction theory
Strikebreakers, 101
Supersedeas bond: required in
  Texaco case, 157–58

Teamsters, International
  Brotherhood of: Local 408,
  109, 110
Texaco: and appeal of damage
  award, 137–42; attempt of to
  acquire Getty Oil, 128–30,
  131, 157; and conflict with
  Pennzoil, 130–34; history and
  development of, 126–27; oil
  reserves problem of, 127–28;
  ordered to pay damages,
  132–34; and partnership
  effort with Standard Oil, 128;
  portrayal of by Pennzoil,
  131–32, 156. *See also* Texaco
  bankruptcy
Texaco bankruptcy, 2, 3, 144,
  185–86; assets after filing,
  146; benefits of, 146, 147, 148,
  154–59; commercial
  creditors' role in, 134–37,
  142–44, 147–48, 153, 154–55,
  169–70, 170–71, 174–75;
  reorganization plan of, 149–
  50, 151, 152–54; and
  settlement with Pennzoil,
  148, 152–53; suppliers' role
  in, 142–43, 155–56; use of
  laws in, 144–46, 147, 158–59.
  See also Texaco
"Texaco Star Theatre," 127
Texas Air Corporation, 120–21.
  See also Texas International
  Airlines

Texas Company. *See* Texaco
Texas International Airlines:
  acquisition of, 88–90;
  attempt of to acquire
  National Airlines, 90; and
  takeover of Continental
  Airlines, 90–93. *See also*
  Continental Airlines; Texas
  Air Corporation
Texas Oil. *See* Texaco
Texas Supreme Court, 142
Thackeray, William, 15
Tort law, 9, 79
Toxic wastes, 3
Transaction cost analysis, 185,
  186–88; of Manville case, 187
Tremain, Israel, 14
Trollope, Anthony, 15
*Turnaround: Avoid Bankruptcy
  and Revitalize Your Company*
  (Friermuth), 3

Union of Flight Attendants, 100
Unions: attempt by to acquire
  Continental Airlines, 92–93;
  and challenge of Continental
  bankruptcy proceedings, 97–
  98, 100; and dispute with
  Continental Airlines, 93–95,
  96, 100, 104–5, 106–9, 115–
  16, 175; early relationship of
  with Continental Airlines,
  83–84; vulnerability of, 118–
  19. *See also* Bildisco case;
  Labor costs
United Airlines, 104
U.S. Commerce Department, 38
U.S. Congress, 28
U.S. Constitution, Art. I, Sec. 8,
  clause 4, 18

U.S. Second Circuit Court: decision in Continental case, 107

U.S. Supreme Court: decision in Continental case, 109, 110–11; decision in Texaco case, 142

Valente, Sal, 110
Valuation process, 185; uncertainty of, 31, 165–67
Value, future, 165, 178
Vanity Fair (Thackeray), 15

Varney Air Transport. *See* Continental Airlines

Wage structure, two-tiered, 104–5
Wagner Act, 112
Warren, Charles, 18, 19, 22
Way We Live Now, The (Trollope), 15
Weil, Gotschal & Manges, 33, 97
Weinstein, Jack, 176
Welfare rights, 107
Winpisinger, William, 112

Compositor: Recorder Sunset Press
Text: 10/13 Aster
Display: Fenice Regular
Printer: Edwards Brothers, Inc.
Binder: Edwards Brothers, Inc.

HG
4061
·D 45
1992

HG
4061
.D45

1992

$23.00